LIVES WORTH LIVING

"WE MUST BE WILLING TO GIVE UP THE LIFE WE HAVE PLANNED SO AS TO APPRECIATE THE LIFE THAT IS WAITING FOR US."

— JOSEPH CAMPBELL

Acknowledgements

To all the people who have supported us financially, you've made this possible. A list of supporters is in the back of the book but there are many others who contributed financially and in kind.

Guy Hayler at **www.crowdfunder.co.uk** for his support and advice.

Matt Ryman of marketing company, **www.spidersandmilk.com** for the video.

Fiona Hennessy, Hennessy Marketing **www.hennessymarketing.co.uk**

Daniel Loveday, book design, **www.daniellovedaycreativesolutions.com**

Alison Shakspeare, editorial, **www.shakspeareeditorial.org**

Allan Benson, **www.thenikonbloke.co.uk**

To all at **Children's Hospice South West** and **Jessie May Trust.**

Together for Short Lives charity for helping to promote the project.

Tori Elliott, cover design, **www.torielliott.com**

Having studied Illustration BA (Hons) at Falmouth, Tori specialised in illustrating children's books and has collaborated with Lou Rhodes with two books, published by Strata Books. Tori has Muscular Dystrophy and in May 2014 she embarked on a tour of Europe to promote independent travel for wheelchair users.

Copyright © Janet Cotter 2014

First published 2014 on behalf of the authors by **Southgate Publishers Ltd**.

Southgate Publishers Ltd, The Square, Sandford, Crediton, Devon EX17 4LW

Printed and bound in Great Britain by Latimer Trend, Plymouth.

British Library Cataloguing in Publication Data

A CIP catalogue record for this book is available from the British Library.

ISBN 9781857411683

Lives Worth Living is dedicated to the children and young people whose short lives are remembered in this book, and to their courageous and resilient families.

Contents

Contents

Introduction

This book deals with a rarely mentioned subject, children with life-limiting conditions. Through true stories, written by brave parents and relations, the reader experiences the joys and the tears, the struggles and the laughter in their daily lives. They take us into a world where every second is precious; where being a carer means being on call day and night, 365 days a year; a world in which the resilience of the human spirit, infused with love, meets every challenge head on.

From the outset, one of those parents, Julie Kembrey, has worked closely with me, giving generously of her time and expertise. She, like all those involved, has found the telling of her story both emotionally challenging and hugely rewarding. This book has been very much a collaborative venture and our aim has been to help others in similar circumstances. Perhaps reading these stories will encourage a more inclusive attitude to the disabled within our community. Professionals too may wish to consider and review their practice in the light of some parents' experiences.

Let's not forget though that, above all else, this is a celebration of short but significant lives; lives that simply make the most of every moment; lives that find happiness in unexpected places and accept what each day brings.

These are powerful stories that cause us to pause and re-evaluate the priorities in our own lives.

Billy-Rose

By Josie

The wonderful adventures of Billy-Rose probably began aeons ago. This time round she joined us through a golden, spirally, love bubble created by Ben and Josie, her dad and mum.

Ben and I had known of each other for years. He was a handsome man and a talented musician. I admired his skills, especially his dedication and talent. I had spent my life exploring this world we live in. I had ventured far and wide, studying the philosophies and healing practices of Eastern cultures, but would always return to England. Once back I would bring these lessons into my life and work with the vulnerable in society. From the first moment Ben and I got together I knew that this was the real thing. So no wonder a soul in search of love and comfort should choose us as her blessed parents.

We had decided to take things gently since we had to sort out our respective lives before totally committing to a life together. Well, that was our plan. However, Billy-Rose obviously had some ideas of her own. She had decided to fling us head first into being a family.

I did the first pregnancy test secretly, under one of my favourite trees down by the river. A ladybird kept me company while I waited for the result. Of course, it was just what I had expected and there was great rejoicing — that is from the tree, the ladybird and me! A previous miscarriage had made me cautious, that and the newness of the relationship. But the next time I saw Ben I was sure he knew as he kept mentioning that he was totally up for a baby should one happen to come along. Me and Billy-

Rose, still keeping our secret, smiled to ourselves.

Some time later Ben and I went off to Bristol to work on an old fishing boat I'd bought. Ben loved fishing, loved boats and had the passion and skill to restore her. At the end of the first week I found the suspense too much and told Ben the good news. We were both so happy, you would have thought we'd won the golden ticket. We sat down and considered a name and agreed on Billy, after Billy Bragg the musician. Ben had played drums for him in the past and there were plans for them to work together in the future.

So, that is where we began; me, Ben and Billy, happily making plans for our lives together. We had to stop working on the boat for a bit — rising costs and rotten hulls scuppered our plans somewhat, but we had others, and Ben kept us upbeat, singing lullabies to help us sleep.

At seven weeks I began my letters to our little Billy. I told her of the changes I was making, the super-healthy eating, clearing out all the junk from my life, protecting her. Ben was following suit, we were both determined to give our baby a healthy start.

The first wobble, and a sign that things may not be going quite as we had planned, came with the scan at 13 weeks. I went with Mum. We dressed up and were very proud and happy to see Billy on the screen, giving us high fives. I love my Mum; she's my best friend and the best companion I could have had for what followed.

We had had a chat with the nurse when we arrived and I had declined the Downs syndrome screening explaining that it wasn't an issue for us as I had previous nursing experience and had worked with loads of wonderful children with all sorts of additional needs, and Mum was a special needs co-ordinator, so we would love this baby however she turned out. How did Ben feel? Simple. Ben loves everyone. Smiles all round.

However, this changed when during the scan they noticed Billy's head was significantly large and took a measurement, 7.2mm. Heads tilted sympathetically towards us, voices were lowered and I was informed that I was now on a different path from the one I wanted to be on. Ben's reaction when I told him there was something wrong was, "In that case we'll just have to love her more to make up for it!"

I had been persuaded to terminate a previous pregnancy and bitterly regretted it. I didn't feel that I had been given all the facts I needed to make a really informed choice. I certainly wasn't told how much support you'll get or how much joy a unique little individual can bring. So that experience convinced me that I would be going ahead with this one, come what may.

I Googled the condition and discovered that a 7.2mm measurement of the nuchal fold was highly significant and, alarmingly, 98% of people terminate on this information alone.

Bath and Bristol hospitals were soon in touch offering tests and advice, but I chose to decline their offers as they all indicated that this was a condition that could not be treated and, therefore, I felt why put Billy through more distress. Clearly there was enough going on for her as it was. I felt the best I could do was to get back on track with loving her every moment we had. I did wobble, I admit, and felt confused and depressed, but with Mum's support I got through it eventually.

Looking back on that time I realise now I was grieving for a life that I had expected to go one way and which was now going in a totally different direction. I remember, too, wondering what my friends' reactions would be. None of them had disabled children. Would I be the only one in my community with a special child? Perhaps people would think I shouldn't have had her. All these doubts and questions ran endlessly round in my head. My life to date had revolved around travelling and working at festivals. I'd had so many adventures but all I wanted now was to settle down and be a mum. Had I left it too late? Was it my fault Billy had these problems? Was I made up wrong? Was I being punished or tested? This was a very hard time for Ben and me but our determination to give Billy a chance at life was never really in question.

Everything changed around Christmas time when I met Ben's family and felt immediately welcome and at home. Ben and I managed to brush aside our worries and focused on each other, basking in the love and support of our two families.

I moved in with my brother Mark and was with him and Palva when their son Aryon was born prematurely. He was healthy but as there were a few problems they spent Christmas and New Year in NICU, our first experience of a place that would later become our 'home'.

Before the 34-week scan Ben and I reiterated our position. We didn't want too much information and, whatever the outcome, we were determined to have our baby. We were happy that we were having a beautiful pregnancy and the rest we would face together, one step at a time.

In my letters to Billy I wrote: "What's the point in finding out about problems they can't do anything about. We'll just keep walking in the woods, singing our songs and dancing our dances."

So we went for the scan with mixed emotions. Mum drove us there and Ben and I sat in the back, clutching each other's hand. He was very shaky, more anxious than he would admit and so was I, but we tried not to show it.

That day changed everything. It was there that it all happened. In the scanning room the Stenographer studied the screen. At first she remarked on the usual things and then appeared rather shaky, saying she would like us to see the Consultant before going any further as there was a real problem. She left us with these thoughts.

On her return she apologised for the fact that there was likely to be a very long wait before we could be seen. We were sent back into the busy waiting room, full of happy, pregnant mothers and their lively offspring. Ben obviously found the waiting and the noise stressful and, after a while, said he was going to go outside for a quiet smoke. I nearly went with him but as an ex-smoker I thought it best to stay where I was; I didn't want to be tempted to join him.

Why, oh why, did I let him go on his own! I have been over and over it in my mind a billion times. If only I'd gone with him, if only …

Time passed and Mum decided she'd had enough of waiting and went off to find someone to sort out what was happening. Alone, I began to feel uneasy about Ben; he'd been away too long and I needed him with me.

As I reached the Reception area I saw a crowd of medics tending to someone lying on the floor. As I got closer I saw to my horror it was Ben. They were helping him up and into a wheelchair. "Let me through. I'm his partner," I cried.

A nurse standing close by commented, "I saw him go down. He had a fit and hit his head on the floor, really, really hard."

Confused and disorientated, he was rushed to A&E while I explained he had had fits before and usually took a while to come round. When I next saw him he was on a bed, wired up to a machine and having more fits. From my basic training I knew that concurrent fits was bad but at that moment a nurse came to take me to the consultant. I reluctantly left Ben, hoping that the doctors would manage to stabilise him by the time I got back.

I must have been in shock because as the consultant spoke to me I felt strangely calm. She explained that Billy was, in fact, a girl, our Billy-Rose, with fully functioning organs, but that her condition was severe and her life expectancy poor. She said we had serious decisions to make. "No, not until I have discussed it with my daughter's father."

Back in A&E a scan had revealed bleeding from the brain and Ben was being sent straight to Frenchay Hospital. I told him not to worry, we were going to be fine and that we loved him, then he was gone.

The following days passed in a blur. I do remember a meeting at the hospital after Ben had slipped into a coma, when the neurosurgeon was describing the impact of the fall and added that if Ben survived he would be seriously brain damaged. The registrar, who was also in the room, asked me questions about the events of that day and when I mentioned Billy-Rose's brain scan results, he turned away and wiped a tear from his eye. Even in my dazed state I remember that compassionate gesture so clearly.

When I think back on it all it felt like a really bad episode of

Casualty, one with a completely ridiculous storyline that no one would believe. Unfortunately for us, it was real.

Meanwhile, Mum was busy researching Billy-Rose's condition. According to the consultant, if she survived the birth she would have an "extremely poor quality of life".

I had briefly considered termination. Phrases like "you don't want her to suffer" are very persuasive, and there was Ben, who had had a serious operation and was now connected to a life-support machine. Wouldn't it be best for him to wake up and know there were no more worries, no more decisions, that we could start all over again? I am pleased to say I did not entertain those thoughts for long. The consultant's words had made me think back to the remarkable individuals I had worked with in the past, many of whom had had very complex needs. Many didn't do the 'normal' things – like talking, walking, going to school, or even growing up – but they still enjoyed a quality of life that, although different, made their lives worth living. I determined I was going to give that chance to Billy-Rose. She had proved she was a fighter and we both deserved to see it through and at least have the experience of a loving birth.

My instincts and some expert advice from Sally, a wonderful midwife friend, led the way! We read stories of parents whose babies, like mine, were life-limited, and their courage shone through. None of them regretted having them and described how life-changing and positive the experience had been.

So here I was, facing the prospect of a severely disabled child, if she made it at all, and, if he pulled through, a severely disabled partner. Well, I had no idea how I was going to cope but I knew I had to give it a go. Although it was an incredibly intense time,

I suppose what gave me the strength I needed was my lively daughter, still growing and merrily kicking away inside me – and a lot of egg mayonnaise sandwiches and cups of hospital canteen tea!

One Sunday night I had a vivid dream. I was sitting down by the river and Ben came by, looking amazingly strong and handsome. We talked and talked but, as he got up to leave, I begged him not to go. He gave me a reassuring kiss, smiled and silently walked away.

That morning I got a call from the hospital. Ben's condition had seriously deteriorated and there was nothing more they could do. Hard as it would be, I needed to let him go.

Friends, and he had loads, and family flocked to say their farewells. I told him how much he was loved and that he had done so well and it was okay to go into the light with love, and rest in peace. For the rest of that day I too was blessed with an immense peace.

That didn't last long and the next day grief hit me like a tidal wave. I felt such anger. I, we, had been cheated, given no time to make memories together like everyone else. There was no consolation; every way I turned I faced a brick wall. No one dared say, "At least you have the baby", because she was going to die too. Normally, when a baby dies friends can say, "You still have each other", but Ben was gone and soon I would be alone. Full of dark thoughts, I felt the only way out would be to follow them. Fortunately, I still had my family and I could never hurt them. So those desperate thoughts were banished from my mind. With the family's help I eventually understood that to survive I needed to grab hold of all the love in the story and let that carry me through.

I was 35 weeks pregnant. The ructions Ben's unexpected death had caused had the midwives leaping into action. At the next meeting they were sympathetic and supportive and arranged for me to see a paediatrician who would answer all my questions. Sally was in touch with a wonderful child bereavement service that gave me the great advice to, "make memories now".

We also contacted the local children's hospice. Could this be a place to go if Billy-Rose made it through the birth? They were super helpful and also attended the meeting with the paediatrician, Bernie. His words changed everything, "She may not hold on to life reliably, but it doesn't take much brain to be a baby."

With this support I went from believing that life was all over to being fully in the moment. Off I went with Val to buy a beautiful first outfit, a babygrow with *Daddy's Little Dreamer* printed on the front. I now knew Billy-Rose and I would meet and I dared to hope she would stay around a while.

Ben's funeral and wake were at this time too and gave me added strength to face the future. Crowds came to show love and celebrate his life. Billy Bragg came and played, which was brilliant, but it was Billy-Rose who helped to keep me strong and calm; she was my guiding force and comfort.

Everyone in my small town got behind us and in wishing us well offered all kinds of help and treatments, homeopathy, counselling, massage, together with very practical help. Sometimes, when I felt lost and alone, I would remember this love and it would tangibly get me through those dark days. It did then, and it still does.

I had organised a home birth. It was to be a joyous occasion come what may, but with the proviso that, if necessary, I could be transferred to hospital. As it turned out that was just as well! Billy-Rose, unsurprisingly, kept us waiting and, as I listened to the CD Ben had created for us, I became increasingly scared that she wasn't alive and recognised I needed to be in hospital. There, with the wonderful Bernie in attendance, she eventually put in a long-awaited appearance. Here she was, alive and kicking! It was the most beautiful moment of my life. Her little eyes winked at me and, for the first time, as I touched her I smelt that gorgeous new baby smell. But then it was off to NICU and an incubator.

Billy-Rose had arrived safely in this world but her fight to stay in it was just beginning. I was to go on a ridiculous rollercoaster of emotions over the next few days and weeks, lurching from euphoria to absolute terror as each new piece of information about her complex condition was revealed. I was allowed to hold her and Anna, a lovely Spanish nurse, would lift her gently out of the incubator and into my arms. We would stay like this for hours, gazing at each other in wonder. Undisturbed, I would sing her songs and tell her stories about me and her dad, tell her how much she was loved and of the life that awaited her outside should she choose to stay. Then she would get tired and turn blue and Anna would quickly pop her back in the incubator. This turning blue was the most normal thing in the world for Billy-Rose. It was to become part of my extreme parenting experience. How on earth was I going to cope?

Anna's wise advice, spoken in her beautiful accent, gave me hope and kept me going: "Love her with all the intensity you can, every moment you have." So that's what I did.

Father's Day found Val and me emotional but proud of Billy-Rose. She had made it and was now one week old! Decisions about her long-term care now had to be made. Either she could continue her life being messed about with day and night or we could opt for, in Bernie's words, "minimal intervention, comfort and care". We chose the latter.

So, it was out of the incubator and into a cot and a funky red babygrow. We thought that this was the beginning of palliative care and that she would be slipping away soon, but no, Billy-Rose was writing her own story and she hadn't got to the end yet!

As her condition stabilised, I took over her care and began to feel like a proper mum at last. Sometimes, I was even able to lead the nurses in the best way to treat her as I was getting to know her so well.

At three weeks old the diagnosis finally came. She had a condition called hydranencephaly. The prognosis was not good, a few months at most.

That was it then. Well, Billy-Rose might not be a 'normal' baby, but she was who she was and she was totally perfect to me. Without a neo-cortex she didn't have to bother with all that thinking and, together with the fact that she didn't cry, was able to be perfectly calm and serene. She also gave everyone who came into contact with her a share of that serenity. All who got close to her were touched by it and came to love and respect her.

For the very first time since our arrival at the Bath hospital, going home was mentioned. This meant my training had to be upped. I'd have to learn to do everything; administer medication, change oxygen and feeding tubes, all scary stuff. It was all systems go to get us home. The preparations were exciting but I was aware of the shadow on the horizon as it dawned on me that we were going home for Billy-Rose to die. I so missed Ben at this time but felt his presence strongly and this made me strong. Time might be short but we were going to make the most of it. We were going home, the two of us, and we had a lot of living to do.

Life began to settle into a routine. Like most babies this revolved around sleeping beside me in the Moses basket Ben had bought for her, feeding and changing. We had open access to the hospital for any time we were worried and a whole host of numbers to call for advice, day or night. So we enjoyed everything we did in a slow and gentle way. She loved bath time and this was followed by her special exercises. Billy-Rose's movements were really slow and delicate but she would kick her legs with rhythmical gusto. We swore she was in training for something very important. Then it was massage time. I got to know every bone, every muscle in her body. I remember the feel of her little shoulder blades as I moved my fingers in circles over her whole body and her head, where now a beautiful swoop of strawberry blond hair was beginning to grow. Then our fashionable babe was dressed in one of her many outfits, crocheted by Mum or bought for her by friends or family, and she was ready to meet the day.

In the afternoons we would play. She would lie with her cousin Aryon on a mat, and enjoy the good life in the sun. We'd maybe go for a picnic by the river, which she loved. She'd watch the sun through the trees, dappling light on our faces. It was here she would be more alert as we listened to the river tumbling over rocks and hear bird song in the trees. If it was raining we'd allow a few raindrops to rest on her face and then go inside to play under an old frame we'd found and turned into a mini-sensory area, with fairy lights to look at, crinkly paper to kick, soft things to touch and jingly things to jingle. If she didn't like something she would screw up her face and switch off; if she did like it she would gaze, focus and gently reach out.

I don't think she was supposed to be capable of doing any of it. Billy-Rose had a condition regarded, by some, as being in a vegetative state, but there is no way that you could say that about her. She responded to, and delighted in, everything around her, leading, what was for her, an utterly fulfilled life.

In the evenings we would relax. Mum would come to help as I was getting very little rest and the night-time feed didn't always go so well because of reflux. As the day drew to a close we'd sing to Billy, whisper goodnight to Ben and all three of us would drift off over the rainbow into sleep.

We got out and about, on excursions into town and to the pub for Grandad's birthday. We must have resembled a mobile chemistry lab as I always carried the oxygen on my back, and people did stare when I did her feed, but no one seemed upset, mostly they were just interested by the heart-shaped fixing tape holding the tubes in place on Billy-Rose's lovely face! Reactions were always positive and I never got any negative comments. Everyone seemed to love her and she seemed to thoroughly enjoy the attention. So we weren't isolated at all. Billy-Rose was, in fact, very popular and we even went to a couple of parties.

Having broken through the darkness into fully (well almost) enjoying our life together, we were about to face another battle. It was not possible to ignore the fact the Billy-Rose's head was getting bigger and the only treatment was to insert a shunt. This meant an operation. The medical team who had so far supported us magnificently were, at first, reluctant to even consider it. However, the Hydranencephaly Society told me that I was my child's advocate and must fight for her. So, some time later, I did get to see a neurosurgeon who said the operation was a possibility but a little risky, however without it the outlook was very grim. There seemed to be no other choice than to go for the operation.

So we ended up in Frenchay, where Ben had died. Ben. I had barely had time to grieve for him and, in a way, was already grieving for Billy-Rose, even though she was still here. I was very aware of the shadows cast by death and loss and my resilience was low. But it was at this time that we made our first visit to the hospice and it changed my outlook completely. I'd thought that it would be a place where it was all about coming to terms with dying. Of course, that is part of the story but it incorporates so much more. They, like us, rejoice in the here and now.

Together with the two grannies, we set about building memories. We spent time in the relaxing sensory room where, for the first time, Billy-Rose reached out and actually held one of the coloured light tubes. It was lovely! We expected nothing of her and when she achieved something like that it was massive and in the picture we took of her, she is smiling her face off. We walked in the gardens, even had a Jacuzzi together, as well as getting loads of practical tips from the staff and meeting other brilliant parents. It was an amazing and timely holiday and we left feeling uplifted and empowered.

The visit to North Devon also coincided with a festival Ben's friends were staging. Billy Bragg was going to play and it was to be in memory of Ben and to raise funds for us. It was great to actually be able to be there and everyone treated us like royalty. We stayed just long enough to meet people and say thank you, and have a little dance. We'd been there, that was the main thing.

Billy-Rose was three months old! We raised a fist in defiance at those who'd been determined we should terminate. Her life was not unworthy and deserved to be lived. I saw changes in her every day, she'd smile and even laugh a little. She was focusing on small things, like dragonflies that came to visit the garden, and smelling the flowers. She had also started to make a beautiful sound when she yawned. Billy-Rose's life was glorious and she and I enjoyed every minute of it.

Being at Frenchay gave us a whole new perspective. Billy-Rose's operation was our main focus but while we were there we met a host of parents, all going through tragic, courageous times. We met many brave children fighting heroically for their lives and became connected with the best part of humanity. We shared our experiences and in doing so gave each other strength.

Our little fighter came through with flying colours and, after a short recuperation in Bath Hospital, we were back home. It had been worth it, Billy-Rose was more alert and looked much more comfortable now that the pressure had been released and her head was back to a more normal size.

We continued our earthly adventures. Time passed. Billy-Rose had slowed its pace, almost to the point where it hardly existed at all. She made each moment precious. My mind was mostly still, my heart was full of love and by noticing her every nuance became more aware of life and nature's subtleties. William Blake described it so well: "The universe in a grain of sand and heaven in a flower."

She had given me the gift of time but now she was getting tired. I knew it. I didn't want to know it, but I did. She was letting me know so that it would not be a sudden shock and, although I prayed to all the gods and dared to hope we would make it through the winter, I knew.

Just before Christmas the doctor suggested we go into hospital to give her one more chance at life. I agreed with him, after all it had by now become our second home.

There, in a room the nurses made beautiful with fairy lights, I held her in my arms, her soft, warm body next to mine, as we'd always been. I'd never known her hold my gaze before, so intently, for so long. It was as if she was looking into my soul.

Sometime later, to the gentle music of a Tibetan chant, Billy-Rose broke free to embark on her final and greatest adventure.

As I wrote this, I had great waves of regrets, doubts and questions. Did I do enough? Did I do too much? Could I have done things differently so that she would still be here today? But I know that this is grief, that given time it will flow away on the tide of acceptance.

It was helpful to hear reassurances from our medical team that I did do all that could be done but, more importantly, that I gave her a beautiful life filled with joy and wonder. A life worth living.

The festive season continued around me after the cremation, concluding with a birthday party for my brother on Twelfth Night. It was only then, when it was all over and everyone left to go back to their normal lives that, sitting on my doorstep one cold January evening, I fully realised it was just me now.

But the story wasn't over; I had to continue the rest of it here on earth as just Josie.

I treasured the recording friends had made of a lullaby Ben had written for Billy-Rose, *Right on Your Side*. It spoke of our hopes and dreams for our life together, on the waterways, fishing, sailing. Well, things were different now, but the love is the same. Nine months later (coincidentally) as I'm writing this, that love is helping me to re-create my life, honouring Ben and Billy-Rose and all that I have learnt. During my time with them I discovered strengths I never knew I had, learnt many new skills and understood fully the joy of life. I now hope to pass some of that knowledge on to others who are going through similar situations and difficulties in their lives.

I have become a baby massage instructor and will be taking this to NICU, the hospice and other Lifetime families, to teach parents the joy, intimacy and precious memories it can create.

The hospital report on Ben's 'unexpected death' included the information that since then they have set up a private room, as I suggested, in which parents receiving bad news connected with a pregnancy, could be given space and privacy. This made me feel better. Related to that, with my friend Mel, I am beginning a campaign to help scan departments impart difficult news more compassionately, with information for parents about all their options and offering support and counselling whichever direction they choose.

My friends have done sponsored unicycle and bicycle rides to raise funds for the hospice and support a local family in need of equipment for their lovely daughter who has cerebral palsy.

Money has also been raised for a crèche in Brazil and this February, just as the darkness was becoming overwhelming, I jumped on a plane to meet Helen who had been such a support to me. We headed to the heart of the Brazilian rain forest and I breathed freely for the first time since that cold January day. It was there that shock ended and grieving began.

Grieving is now part of my life and the best thing I have learnt about it, with the help of those around me, is that it comes from love and that is the reason it feels so immense.

This is a true love story and in writing it I trust I have given you some indication of the joy as well as the sadness that Ben and Billy-Rose brought into my life and the lives of all those who were blessed to be part of their story.

THERE IS NO FOOTPRINT
TOO SMALL TO LEAVE AN IMPRINT
ON THIS WORLD.

A Letter To Rachael

By Kate and Sam

Rachael was born in 1991, followed by her brother Sam just over two years later. We felt blessed and happy; our family complete. However, maybe it was a 'mother's intuition' or experience of working with children, but we knew something wasn't quite right. Rachael seemed to be late in reaching most of the 'normal' milestones. It wasn't until she was four years old however, having seen various specialists and after she had lost her sight that we had a diagnosis. It was devastating - not only was our daughter blind but she had a brain tumour.

Rachael gave us fourteen and a half years of joy and laughter. She died peacefully in May 2006.

Dear Rachael,

It is easy for us as your parents and family to appreciate how wonderful you were as a daughter and sister, grandchild, niece and cousin.

You were funny, full of laughter and love. A girl who adored to meet new people and loved to tell jokes. You loved new experiences, rides on roller coasters and going to school! You also loved Sixties music, the colour blue, cats (in particular blue cats!), chocolate, ham sandwiches and cake!

Rachael, you were intensely loyal and hated unfairness in the world (although you never once complained about being ill). To you, everyone was equal. Because you could not see, the colour of a person's skin was unimportant. When you met someone, it really didn't matter how important or how lowly they were, or what clothes they wore, that person was somebody new to talk to.

You were diagnosed with a brain tumour at the age of four, by which time you had already become completely blind. You also had some learning difficulties and later on, at the age of 13, developed epilepsy as a result of extensive surgery. You endured a year of chemotherapy at the age of five and underwent many operations, as well as numerous hospital visits. It wasn't the kind of family life we had imagined for ourselves, or for you. And yet we did try to strive for a life as 'normal' as we could make it for you and your brother. We still expected you to behave well and show good manners; you attended mainstream primary school and we went to church and you attended Sunday school. You especially loved going to Rainbows, Brownies and Guides, although you needed some help for these activities.

We went on family holidays and have wonderful memories of you and Sam, your brother, enjoying so many different experiences. A special trip was seeing your face light up when you met the 'real' Father Christmas in Lapland, feeling his beard and red suit!

When you were 11 you went on a school residential trip to Heatree, an outdoor activity centre. You amazed everybody with your courage and determination – being blind did not stop you, Rachael, from kayaking, climbing, crawling through mud on the assault course and generally having a wonderful time!

You left an enduring legacy Rachael. Members of the congregation had, over the days preceding the service we held to celebrate your life, written their thoughts and memories of you on cut-out hand shapes (because you explored the world with your hands, of course!) and mounted them on a display.

Without exception, everybody had written about your smile and how happy you always looked.

Rachael, one of your special friends was Bishop Bill, who was Bishop of Truro and had first met you on a school visit. At your service of remembrance he gave the address. Here are some of the things he said:

> *All of us have people we carry around inside us. I don't mean the obvious important people like family … I mean people who are in a sense special … inhabit our minds and our hearts in a particular way. People who are quite literally unforgettable. For me Rachael was one of those … She had a quality, a gaiety, an enjoyment of life, in spite of her illness … I loved to see her in the playground surrounded by her friends. Somehow her blindness, immensely sad though it was, didn't seem to matter. She communicated an enjoyment of life which people who knew her just shared because of her. It is easy to measure life by the length of time we live, but life in the end is about the giving and receiving of love. Measured and seen in this way, Rachael's life has been full.*

So you see Rachael, you touched the lives of so many people. You are no longer here in body but you are forever in our minds and thoughts. Much of what we think, and how we act, has been shaped by you. Many of the friends we have made over the years have been because of you. Your lasting legacy to us has been to help us to realise that every day is precious and that we need to live and love life to the full.

With all our love, Rachael

Mum, Dad and Sam xxx

A letter from her brother, Sam.

Dear Rachael,

What is 'normal'? Normal for me is what I've been used to; it's what feels natural. The first twelve years of my life were with you, and I never knew any different. So now, nearly eight years later, I've had to get used to a whole different life without you physically here, and that's not been easy. When you left us in May 2006, all of us in the family had a shock at how different everyday life was without you. You made it special.

So how was my life with you 'normal'? We grew up together closely. You were born two years before me, my big sister. Mum told me how curious you were about having a new baby brother. It was just after I was born, you completely lost your sight and were diagnosed with an optic glioma. You also had learning difficulties. Even though Mum and Dad tried their very best to help and keep your upbringing as 'normal' as it could be, it was difficult. In and out of hospital for reasons I didn't know and probably wouldn't have understood anyway. All I knew was that you were poorly. Despite that, to me it was 'normal'. I got used to it.

You went to primary school and made friends as any other child would. Your disability didn't seem to matter to anyone who met you.

Our holidays I will never forget; going abroad to France, Switzerland, Ireland, Lapland. We had great holidays. Doing things other people do. You didn't let your disability stop you. This was apparent on other outings too, such as school trips. When you got back you couldn't stop talking about your adventures, climbing, assault course activities, you loved them all. I remember too our walks on Dartmoor and around Cornwall and Devon — we did so much.

You taught me not to judge others on their appearance or views. You made me understand what living with a disability is like. Trust was a main point there. The fact that you trusted me made me feel so honoured – I remember some times when we were out shopping or on a walk, you would hold on to my arm and I would lead you. Some people stared because you had a cane and couldn't see where you were going. I remember all the emotions at times like these. I wasn't angry with those people, I was more upset and disappointed because they didn't know you, and were judging you. They didn't understand; to me, you were 'normal'. If these passing people were to meet you, they would have found a kind, caring person, who always thought of others.

I couldn't have wished for anyone else to be my sister. Now that you're not here with us I feel like a part of me has gone too.

I am proud to call you my sister, and when I meet new people and they ask if I had any siblings, I proudly say, "yes". I could talk for hours about you and the things we did, but people seem to think 'passing on' is taboo; they seem to want to move away and talk about something else. So instead, I talk to you, to Mum and Dad, to family and my close friends.

If I could do it all again, I would, but on one condition, your illness didn't cause you any pain. Your constant headaches on top of the epilepsy made me feel so sad because I couldn't relieve your pain. I felt helpless. I only wish you'd spent a longer time at Little Bridge. The short time you had at the hospice was beneficial to both you and me. This was a place where I could talk about my feelings, where you were looked after, and where Mum and Dad could relax too. The on-going support has made a huge difference to how we cope with you not being here. I have someone to talk to about you who really understands.

I don't think I'd be half the person I am now, if you hadn't touch mine, and so many other lives.

I don't like the word 'normal' – because 'normal' means different things to different people. I'd rather call our lives together 'special'.

In a way you're still here, Rachael, and you always will be. Until we meet again,

Sam. Xx

Sam is now at College studying Photography.

LOVE IS THIS
THAT YOU LIVED AMONGST US THOSE
FEW YEARS
AND TAUGHT US HOW TO LOVE.

LOVE IS THIS
THAT YOU DIED AMONGST US AND HELPED US
TO THE SOURCE OF LIFE, LOVE.

Francesca and Josephine

When I was a little girl I loved to play with my dolls. I suppose even then I was preparing for motherhood. As I grew into a young woman my expectations developed further – I planned to go to college, get a job, meet 'Mr Right' and have a family. My life was mapped out in my head and everything seemed to be on course. I passed my exams and found a decent job. When I met and later married Chris everything seemed to be falling into place. After a few blissful years together I became pregnant with twins. Then Francesca and Josephine were born and life WAS perfect. They were absolutely beautiful. We were a family.

It certainly didn't enter my head that our gorgeous girls were carrying the genetic code of a life-limiting disease.

Life can change in a moment. For our family that moment came when our twin daughters, Francesca and Josephine, were diagnosed with a life-limiting illness aged 3½. Prior to this we were an ordinary family with two young children. The girls were lively, cheeky and funny and our days were hectic and happy.

We knew that Fran and Jo had a few developmental problems, including delayed speech, difficulties around toileting and they were less agile than their peers, but none of this seemed very serious because they were always so full of life. It was only when the girls started mainstream nursery, shortly after their third birthday that it became clear they were lagging behind and failing to achieve age-related milestones.

Fran and Jo enjoyed nursery but proved to be a bit of a challenge for the staff. Chris and I were called to the Head Teacher's office on more than one occasion and Josephine was even suspended from nursery for 'unreliable toileting'! We just couldn't understand where we were going wrong. We had always given the girls so much time, attention and encouragement. Why were they having these problems? Were we useless parents?

Fran and Jo's poor performance at nursery triggered a series of assessments and medical tests, including an appointment with the school doctor at the local medical centre. Chris and I experienced quite a lot of stress and frustration at this time but we had no concept of the implications. We felt sure that input from therapists and some extra support at nursery would help the girls to catch up. Even when we were called to an appointment with a paediatrician at the local hospital, we were not particularly worried. We saw it as a step towards sorting out some of the girls' problems.

Little did we know. We were so naïve.

February 15th 1995 started as an unremarkable day. The appointment at the children's centre was set for mid afternoon. When we arrived it was quiet and calm and a member of staff was on hand to play with Fran and Jo while we were called to speak with the doctor. He only had a quick look at the girls. I remember him mentioning a blood test and watched as he carefully applied cream to their chubby hands in preparation. Looking back, the very quick appointment, the quiet environment and short examination time should have given us a clue, but no alarm bells rang at the time. We were totally unprepared for the devastating diagnosis that followed.

The paediatrician was kind, gentle and clear as he told us that our beloved children had a condition called Sanfilippo disease, a genetic, progressive condition and that they were not expected to live to adulthood.

I can remember saying, "That can't be right. They're our only children. They're our whole family." Then I just remember feeling cold, sick with shock.

Details of the rest of the day are very sketchy, but the doctor was wonderful and handled everything with great sensitivity. He handed us a leaflet about the MPS Society, which dealt with this disease, and urged us to contact them for information and support. He arranged a cup of tea for us and a few minutes alone. Finally, we were introduced to a social worker.

As we were reunited with our boisterous children, bright and smiley from an afternoon's play, as always, we were too stunned to even shed a tear.

We had to drive home separately, as Chris had come from work. I have no idea how I drove the car that day, I was completely numb. Chris's brother came home with him and sat with Fran and Jo while we cried and hugged each other in the kitchen. Later on, or the next day, Chris contacted the MPS Society and they have been an important part of our lives ever since. The Society organises regional clinics, quarterly magazines and annual conferences, as well as offering telephone and advocacy support to families whose children are affected by MPS and related diseases.

The days and weeks following the diagnosis are a blur. There was shock, fear and panic. We thought that everything would change straight away and that our lives would collapse around us at any moment.

We decided to be honest and upfront with everyone, so we did the rounds of family and friends, giving our bleak news, spreading sorrow, pain and shock as we went. I felt a complete failure. Our children had inherited this cruel disease from us. Crying doesn't begin to describe the primal howling released in overwhelming waves night after night while Fran and Jo slept peacefully.

Following the diagnosis, there must have been a whole series of appointments and introductions, but I can't recall anything specific, except a home visit by Christine Lavery, founder of the MPS Society. She came to talk to us about Sanfilippo and what to expect. She was sympathetic, but also calm and reassuring, giving well-informed answers to our many questions. That meeting told us we were not the only ones going through this terrible experience. She also arranged an appointment for us with a leading specialist at the Willink Centre, part of Manchester Children's Hospital.

After a few days (possibly even a couple of weeks) we realised that Francesca and Josephine were exactly the same cheerful, funny toddlers. They were still beautiful and precious and we loved them. They hadn't changed at all.

The facts remained the same; the girls would suffer a devastating loss of skills and declining health. They were not expected to live beyond their teenage years. We all had a difficult time ahead of us. But, Fran and Jo were still active and full of life and they needed us to be good parents. We had to make the most of every precious moment with them.

Chris and I made a decision to throw ourselves into giving Fran and Jo the best life we possibly could. We had a plan. We were a team, a gang of four. Together we would make the most of every day. The girls needed us and we didn't want to let them down.

From that point onwards, with a clear objective, we set about our task. We went out and about at every opportunity and whatever the weather. Fran and Jo loved going on all sorts of outings and spending time with family and friends. They adored the beach and splashing in the sea. We bought a cheap dinghy and Jo enjoyed nothing more than jumping from it into the water, secure in the knowledge that, as she couldn't swim, we would pull her to safety. Fran was less adventurous. She liked to pull the little boat along the shoreline with Chris sitting in it.

We took the girls on long walks, finding interesting things to do as we went. They were full of fun and could run really fast if something caught their attention; for Fran this was often food related. On more than one occasion she 'acquired' a bag of crisps from a passing child (we always returned them). For Jo, it was anything that would cause mischief, usually running away or throwing things. She had very little speech, but one of her favourite phrases was, "Oh dear, big trouble", always followed by a fit of giggles. The girls had a knack of running in separate directions so we always needed to know who we were 'marking'. We were constantly on the go, laughing, singing together and making up silly games. Our camera was always at hand so that we could record everything. No outing or achievement was too small to warrant a number of photographs. These were often chaotic or out of focus because the girls were never still, but there were plenty of good ones as well.

When we were at home together, we liked to cuddle up and read stories or watch TV. Fran and Jo couldn't get enough of Disney films, often sitting together, with snacks and drinks, surrounded by books and totally engrossed. They loved hats and dressing up. Their favourite characters were Peter Pan and John from the Disney film. They often went out dressed accordingly. Fran used to say, "Follow me, I'm Peter Pan."

A wonderful freedom came from living life on the girls' terms. Doing the things they loved and living for the moment. They were fantastic, always giggling and finding new ways to be naughty. They were definitely double trouble. For Chris and me there was an urgency about everything we did with our daughters, knowing we couldn't afford to wait or plan ahead. We appreciated every minute.

I have to admit there were days when life was difficult. Fran and Jo were big girls with boundless energy. It wasn't unusual for them to have temper tantrums or to fight and throw toys at each other. They were physically strong and determined to get their own way. Sometimes I questioned my ability to cope. The daily routine was exhausting and repetitive. I had some dark days when I felt lonely, isolated and weepy. Everywhere we went I saw healthy children to remind me of our girls' uncertain future. Sometimes I was overwhelmed by the enormity of our situation.

Luckily for me, Chris is a solid and steady character. His attitude was, "This is the way things are and we have no option but to get on with it." His supportive and pragmatic attitude enabled me to pick myself up and carry on. Then I would look at Fran and Jo and be overcome by my love for them.

The girls' ability peaked at the age of five and in September 1996 they moved from mainstream education to a local school for children with additional needs. At first, Chris and I struggled with the fact that the girls needed special provision, but Fran and Jo were totally at home from day one. It was a perfect environment for them. Instead of being seen as naughty and disruptive, their exuberance was celebrated and encouraged.

As the girls' needs increased, our family required help and support to maintain a good quality of life. Two very special charities became extremely important to us:

> Little Bridge House, a children's hospice in North Devon, where we went for short breaks as a family three or four times a year. Fran and Jo were well cared for and thoroughly spoilt, while Chris and I had a chance to catch up on sleep and recharge our batteries for a couple of days. It was a haven where we could find time and space for ourselves or socialise with other families.

> Jessie May, Children's Hospice at Home, Bristol. This wonderful local charity offered regular, three-hour home visits. This enabled me to leave the house to run errands or meet a friend while the girls were entertained and cared for by highly trained, yet friendly nurses. Jessie May Family Fun Days and Christmas parties were highlights of our year.

Without these two very special charities I'm not sure how we would have coped. Not only did they offer practical support, but also medical advice and someone to talk to about our worries and concerns regarding Fran and Jo. They also offered us the chance to meet other families with similar problems. The value of this cannot be quantified and has lead to some strong and lasting friendships.

Francesca and Josephine lived life at a very fast pace, and with very little sleep until they were nine or ten. At this point they started to experience a devastating loss of skills. Often this was not a steady decline, but a series of massive changes. They slowed down and needed an ever-increasing array of equipment and care. As they were prone to falling, they needed constant supervision. We could feel time slipping away.

It's almost impossible to explain what it feels like to witness your own children losing skills. To me it seemed like stepping off a cliff and not knowing where the next ledge was. Free falling into inky blackness, stomach churning and desperate.

For Chris and me it presented a challenge. How long could we maintain a good quality of life for our daughters? We had promised to do our best so we had to get on with it. We didn't want to let them down or have any regrets when it was too late.

Of course, we had to reduce our expectations, but these had always been based on Fran's and Jo's abilities, so we were already used to that. We bought an adapted minibus in preparation for the girls travelling in wheelchairs. This made a big difference. When Fran and Jo were well enough we took them on outings at weekends and during school holidays. We found new places to visit with easy access. We continued to take them on caravan holidays, packing everything, including mattresses, into the van. This was an exercise in logistics and Chris and I were always exhausted before we'd even left home. But it was always worth the effort and even when the girls were in their mid teens, they still responded to the smells and sounds of the seaside. It was hard work but definitely worth it. Now we have fantastic memories and photographs and we look back at those times with fondness and pride.

Francesca and Josephine were beautiful. Both of them had dark hair, full lips, flawless skin and expressive eyes. Francesca could un-nerve people with her unwavering eye contact. Her calm and steady gaze made you feel that she was looking into your heart and soul. She valued her personal space, viewing newcomers from a cool distance until she decided whether they were worth engaging with.

Josephine's personality was quite different. She was open and friendly with everyone. She loved new people, especially when they gave her lots of attention. Jo was funny, cheeky and boisterous. She was always laughing. To her, anything could be turned into a game.

As they got older Fran and Jo suffered a greater loss of skills and failing health, but they did not lose their spirit. Even as a teenager, Fran still proved to be a good judge of character so we observed her body language when selecting carers. Jo always enjoyed being around people, especially when they were good fun and she was the centre of attention.

Both our girls were comfortable with who they were. They didn't ever seem to be embarrassed or shy. They took everything in their stride. It's a lesson I am trying to learn from them – with limited success so far.

Our boundless love for our beautiful girls and the determination and zest for life they both possessed was no match for Sanfilippo disease.

Francesca died at home in February 2007, aged 15½.

Josephine died at Little Bridge House in December 2009, aged 18½.

We miss them both every single day and cherish the years they shared with us so generously. We laugh and cry when we look at photos of them, as precious memories come flooding back. We will carry our love for Francesca and Josephine in our hearts forever as they continue to influence our decisions and values.

It is impossible to explain what it feels like to lose a child. Part of me died with my children, leaving a cold, empty space that can never be filled. When Francesca died at home in February 2007, our whole family was devastated. I remember feeling sick and cold all the time. It seemed unreal, like a bad dream.

However, we were still Josephine's parents and she needed all of our love and attention. Not only was she fragile and profoundly disabled, but she had also lost her twin sister. Josephine gave us the strength and purpose to carry on. Somehow, we put our grief 'on hold' so that we could care for Jo, but there was more to it than that. Josephine looked like Francesca, she even adopted some of Fran's traits. For example, she changed her habit of snuggling under the bedding and started sleeping with her arms out of the covers, as her sister had always done. It was as if Francesca was still around.

People used to ask if Josephine missed her sister, but she showed no signs of distress. Maybe they still had some connection? Or perhaps Jo assumed Fran was around somewhere. We showed her photographs of Francesca and talked about her all the time.

In many ways Josephine thrived on the undivided attention she was receiving for the first time in her life. Josephine continued to go to school with 1:1 support until she became seriously ill in October 2007. Somehow she pulled through with steely determination, but from then on her health was too fragile and unpredictable for her to return to the busy school environment. Her 1:1 support transferred to home during school hours and she enjoyed a calmer lifestyle. Jo was often well enough to go out and about, but everything was done at her pace. Even meetings and health reviews took place in our home. Our house was always busy with family members, carers and health professionals. Josephine was at the centre of a very large team and it was my job to co-ordinate them all on her behalf. There was never enough time, but it was a happy and well-organised routine. The stress and worry around Jo's health and care needs was tempered with laughter, music and chatter as we all did our best to keep her happy, comfortable and entertained. We all adored her.

In November 2009, during one of our planned visits to Little Bridge House, Josephine developed a severe chest infection. Despite everyone's best efforts, Jo died at the hospice in December 2009.

To me it felt like both our girls died that day. Josephine had represented her sister as well as herself in our daily routine. Her soft and gentle presence had given comfort and purpose. There was nothing better than sitting with her, holding hands or giving her a cuddle.

In a moment everything was gone. The house fell silent. My life had no focus. I was no longer a mum. I lost confidence and felt totally isolated, even though Chris and I had wonderful support from our family and friends. The life I had lived for almost 20 years vanished. I had no idea how to carry on. My body was numb and cold, as if my insides had turned to stone.

Most of the people who had frequented our house over the years had been the girls' network, not mine. Although I had always understood this, the reality of the emptiness was shocking. I also realised that I would no longer be meeting other parents via Jessie May Family Events or at Little Bridge House. This compounded my feelings of loss and isolation.

From the day Francesca and Josephine received their diagnosis we had been grieving for the life we had expected but did not have. But our unexpected life was busy and full of unconditional love and rich experiences. It bore no comparison to our feelings when our gorgeous girls died.

I wanted to meet other bereaved parents, but how?

The girls and I had received wonderful care in the form of homeopathy and counselling from The Rainbow Centre in Bristol and this continued for me after their deaths.

Chris and I were also receiving bereavement support from Jessie May and the children's hospice in the form of home visits and telephone support, but I wanted something more. The 1:1 visits were helpful, but they made me feel needy and vulnerable. I wanted to have some independence around my grief and I wanted to know how other bereaved parents were coping. I approached Jessie May with an idea for a peer/friendship group for bereaved parents. I must have made a decent case since they agreed to give it a try as long as I was prepared to commit my time and effort into the development and running of the group. I worked alongside Jessie May bereavement staff to come up with a plan and the Purple Group was formed. All administration and contact with parents is done by Jessie May staff, but I am involved in planning and running the sessions with them. Through the Purple Group, Chris and I have met inspirational parents who are struggling with grief, just as we are. We can share our stories and emotional responses openly and honestly, without being pitied. What a relief!

One of the things we have learnt from the group is that bereaved parents want to talk about the child/children they have lost, but doing so often causes embarrassment and awkwardness to others.

As a bereaved mum I sometimes feel that I am viewing life through a window. I can see what's going on and I can be seen, but I am an outsider because of my loss. For this reason it has been hugely beneficial for me to find a peer group. It has given me confidence and a new perspective. I can be myself.

Of course, life is still a challenge as we try to find our way forward without our children. Anniversaries are the hardest times, and we find ourselves under a dark cloud. Chris and I have developed a strategy for dealing with these difficult days. We spend the day together doing something Francesca and Josephine would have enjoyed, usually an outing or a long walk involving a meal or a picnic. This gives us a chance to remember the lovely times we all shared together and to celebrate our daughters' lives.

Francesca and Josephine were our only children and I was determined to find a way of keeping them in my life after they died. I started volunteering with the Jessie May Team helping them raise much-needed money by telling our story to enhance various funding bids and conferences. In July 2013, Jessie May were invited to a reception at No.10 Downing Street, hosted by Samantha Cameron, where I had the honour of speaking about Francesca and Josephine, as well as the Purple Group. It was a truly memorable day and, somehow, I didn't feel particularly daunted or nervous. The girls were with me and I was telling others about the value of their lives and the fact that, in spite of the heartache, there was joy and that they had made every day worth living.

So this is where I am, where we are now, but who knows where our girls will lead us in the future. We will have to wait and see.

"WHEN WE ARE DEAD AND PEOPLE WEEP
FOR US AND GRIEVE,
LET IT BE BECAUSE WE TOUCHED THEIR
LIVES WITH BEAUTY AND SIMPLICITY.

LET IT NOT BE SAID THAT LIFE
WAS GOOD TO US BUT RATHER
THAT WE WERE GOOD TO LIFE."

JACOB P. RUDAN

Bethany Joy

Beautiful, courageous and inspirational

Born 21st April 1998 by emergency caesarian following inducement lasting two days.

We had been sent home the previous day as the booking system had been mucked up and my name wasn't down. I don't think any staff even looked at my notes, or asked me any questions to assess any distress this may have caused, and I had no experience of what to expect.

There was quite a history on me already by then, the reason being that, at an eleven-week scan, a nuchal translucency was detected (a thickening in the back of the neck). I was told at the scan that this is often related to a type of syndrome. I was monitored weekly from then on with scans, with me repeatedly asking if I could have further tests. Deep down, I knew there was a problem, despite any and every practitioner telling me everything was going to be fine. Not feeling I was being heard, and relying on and trusting the confident medics, was a very early learning curve for me.

I use the word practitioner, rather than expert or professional, as it was me who knew and felt that things weren't right when I was pregnant with my beautiful daughter Bethany Joy, not any of the 'professionals' who saw me in clinic. Recognising my expertise and the bond I had with Bethany Joy became the most powerful tools for both of us throughout her short and precious life.

I can remember being put on a ward of mothers with healthy

newborn babies. I was left with a Polaroid picture by my bed, having had just a glimpse of my precious Bethany before she was rushed off to the children's hospital to prepare for surgery on her bladder, which was on the outside of her body when she was born.

I felt distraught that I could not be with her. All my dreams of holding her in my arms and feeding her were stripped from me. Instead, I was questioned by other new mums as to where my baby was.

Eventually, having self discharged, I got to Bethany's incubator where I could only sit and watch her, her legs bandaged together following her operation. At this point I was pushed away and a form was handed to me about applying for disability benefits. I had had it in my mind that, as soon as her bladder was fixed, she would be fine and we could go home to begin our lives together and then I could become her mummy.

I was still in denial about Bethany having any significant disability, even when the geneticist spoke about a possible chromosomal abnormality. There had been tests during my pregnancy to rule this out, so I felt confident that they would still come back as 'normal'. I continued to be in denial, even when she told me Bethany did have this unique abnormality. She explained that this meant no one would be able to predict her outcome in terms of any disability.

After a couple of months in neo-natal care within the children's hospital, we were discharged. I was terrified! I was already completely institutionalised; it felt like I was stealing this little precious special baby away from the hospital without any qualifications to look after her.

At home, I spent all my time trying to appease Bethany's cries of distress and constant sickness, day and night. We also had a barrage of clinic appointments with neurology, genetics, urology, nephrology, ophthalmology, ears, nose and throat, and cardiology, to name but a few. Yet, when I did fill in a disability benefits form and ask my GP to support my application, I was turned down. The reason given? That maybe there was nothing wrong with Bethany. Fortunately, I found an ally in Bethany's geneticist, who wrote to the benefits agency, and Bethany was finally awarded benefits for life.

Confused, scared and angry, I withdrew from everything and chose to spend all my time with Bethany. I began to play with her, sing and chat to her, massage her hands and feet and carried her everywhere in a baby sling, desperately trying to get some reaction from her. One day, she was lying in my bed, where I could see her while I changed the cover on the duvet. I flapped the duvet cover over her face and said, "Peek a boo!" She reacted with a little laughing sound. I couldn't believe it, so I repeated it over and over again and each time she responded with a little laugh.

At last I had found my beautiful Bethany Joy!

In an instant I was given the strength to be with her every moment of her precious little life within this world. I wanted to be there for her, no matter what was thrown at us. She would come first, forever and always.

Sadly, throughout our journey together she was in constant pain. She had to endure many life-threatening hospital admissions, often resulting in long stays in intensive care. I'm still angry about this because I feel that if only I could have been stronger and questioned the many professionals/experts, and listened to my gut feeling, so many of the admissions could have been avoided.

In her first year, the only communication I had with the outside world was at hospital or with family and two close friends. All other friends and work colleagues had dropped off the radar. I remember being so terribly shocked when a family member asked, "Do you intend to have more children?" I was in a state of shock and surprise. Since Bethany's birth I had felt like a complete alien and had isolated myself from the rest of the world. This was a different reality and this new 'normal' made me hurt so much inside. I could not imagine that others would see me as 'normal' ever again and certainly not as someone who would be able to go on and have another child. But this comment did trigger a glimmer of hope. It did much to move me into a new phase where I was able to take an interest in shaping a life for myself, with Bethany in it.

I had a wonderful relationship with Bethany's geneticist and felt I could have frank discussions about the possibility of another pregnancy. Since her father and I had normal chromosomes there was no reason why we shouldn't go on to have a non-disabled sibling for Bethany.

My love for, and unquestionable commitment and dedication to, my beautiful and precious daughter continued to grow every moment of every day, despite the need for constant management of her pain, sickness, food intake and medication. This regime led to complete exhaustion but, knowing that the pain I suffered was mainly emotional, I was able to get through it because I knew my little angel was in constant, excruciating physical pain.

After eighteen months of Bethany's life, her baby sister Amelia was born. This was to be the biggest and best turning point in Bethany's life. While she had been locked away in her painful body, trying to make sense of the world, her little sister gave her no choice but to interact.

This was, without doubt, the most beautiful bond I have had the privilege to witness. Amelia, at the age of nine months, could walk and talk and eat. Bethany was unable to achieve any of these. Amelia adored her sister and included her in all her play. She could tell anyone who walked into our home, why Bethany was reacting in a certain way, why she was hurting and, most importantly, what to do about it.

The feeling was mutual. Bethany never formally communicated, but somehow our little family unit grew to know her noises, her painful looks, her little movements. Most obvious was her love for her little baby sister.

Our lives revolved around endless hospital stays all over the country. Selflessly, from the word go, Amelia would choose to be by Bethany's bedside. She sang away, delighting in the reactions she got from her special sister, which encouraged her to perform more.

Right up to the moment Bethany drifted away forever on 14th December 2009, Amelia was beside her, singing to her and telling her how much she loved her.

As a mum, I can only speak of what a privilege it was, and is, to have experienced this unique and wonderful journey with my two beautiful daughters. I feel I have an understanding and outlook on life that has only been possible because of Bethany Joy.

Amelia – a special sister

Who made me laugh when I was in the bath by singing and dancing – Amelia

Who never complained when I sat in front of the television – Amelia

Who made my swing go really high to make me giggle – Amelia

Who sang to me on the telephone when I was sad in hospital – Amelia

Who made me laugh when she made my chair go round and round – Amelia

Who kept talking to me in hospital although I was not conscious – Amelia

Who splashed me in the bath when we were together to make me laugh- Amelia

Who recorded songs on my button to make me happy when we were apart – Amelia

Who helped Mummy whenever she was needed at all times – Amelia

Who swam round and round very fast in the hot tub to make me laugh – Amelia

Who banged our bikes together when we went on a cycle ride – Amelia

Who put her arms around me on the beach to keep me warm – Amelia

Who told Grandma what to do when I was in her house – Amelia

Who always included me in every way just to keep me happy – Amelia

Who pushed me round and round on my roundabout – Amelia

Who even wiped my nose and mouth for me – Amelia

Who fed me in the car when we were travelling – Amelia

Who loved me very, very much – my special sister – Amelia x

SHE WOULD COME FIRST,
FOREVER AND ALWAYS.

Jo and Amelia

Andrew and Martin

By Nicola

This is the story of two brothers. Normal boys in every way except that, for most of their lives, they used wheelchairs instead of legs.

It was on my 25th birthday that I learnt of Andrew's condition. He was then six years old and, once the consultant had looked at his over-developed calves, I was told he was suffering from Duchennes muscular dystrophy, whatever that was. One thing was for certain, he would end up in a wheelchair.

So, those who had predicted "with legs like that he'll make a great rugby player" were wrong.

Stunned into silence by the details of the diagnosis, and thinking the consultation was over, I headed for the door. But, before I could leave, the consultant added, "If you have other sons, they would probably have it too." He was obviously unaware of the existence of Martin, Andrew's lively, four-year-old brother. My heart sank.

"Thank you," I replied, and left.

As I stood outside the hospital letting his words sink in, I realised that the life I'd had when I left the house this morning was not the one I would now return to. For all of us everything had changed.

What to do? Well, we did have a choice. We could either cave in or fight. We all decided to fight.

I had always wanted boys and four seemed a good number. When Andrew was born in 1983 he was perfect and I was over the moon! A contented baby, he seemed to do everything right; he even walked at eleven months! When two years later Martin came along to join him I was thrilled. He too seemed a normal baby, although he didn't walk until he was eighteen months old, but this didn't worry me at the time. I was just comparing him with his brother so I didn't think any more about it.

As Andrew grew he developed really big calf muscles and fell over a lot. He also struggled to ride a bike. I just thought he was clumsy, like me. At playschool he had been fine, no one noticed anything wrong. But when he went to school and had his first medical, the doctor was concerned by the size of his calves and he was referred to a specialist at the hospital.

That was when we realised life wasn't going to be easy.

I determined that my boys would live their lives to the full, come what may. I wanted them to be 'normal' and do all the things other boys do, however hard it might be. They still went to school, still had friends, and were still the little buggers they had always been. The diagnosis hadn't changed that. So it was up to me to juggle life around so that we could fit in their many hospital appointments, and all the other stuff we'd have to contend with, and still have time for fun.

We chose to go to Hammersmith Hospital, as this was reputedly the best place for treating their condition. It was a terribly long journey from Redruth in Cornwall to London, but it had to be done. We used to have to leave at six in the morning to catch the train and, even if everything went smoothly, didn't return until after ten at night. A very long day.

I did not intend for them to die because of me and, therefore, I tried my best to put into practice every bit of advice they gave us at the hospital.

These trips always turned into an adventure, worrying at the time but funny afterwards. Once, Martin and I had to stay overnight at the hospital and waking, as I always did, to check on him in the night, I found his bed empty. I panicked and so did the staff. We rushed about the ward, searching in and out of day rooms, hunting for a missing child who had mysteriously escaped! I was frantic with worry. Finally, exhausted, I returned to our room. It was then that I noticed the bulge at the end of his bed and turning back the covers found Martin, wrapped up like a pancake roll under the blankets, still fast asleep. I could have killed him, and so could the nursing staff.

It was particularly difficult if I had both the boys with me. On one such trip we got to the station to return home and we were told that all the trains were cancelled. A horrendous journey on buses and taxis followed. When we finally got back to the house in the small hours, all completely shattered, we decided that was it, in future we'd go to Treliske, in Cornwall, instead. Fortunately, they were equally good to us and soon grew to love my naughty boys. Everyone seemed to warm to us, maybe because, in spite of everything, we always saw the funny side.

One of the difficult times was Andrew's first operation to release the tendons in his heels. This was done to help him stay mobile for as long as possible. He left hospital with full leg calipers to help him walk. He had to stand for a long time in these calipers as part of the recovery treatment and I had to do physiotherapy on his legs. It was really painful and hard work for us both, but it worked for a while. However, both boys went off their legs when they were nine years old.

They still enjoyed school where they had helpers and seemed to cope okay with everything. They were popular and had lots of friends, which was lovely, and were always accepted for who they were and not because people felt sorry for them.

One time Andrew's teacher nominated him for a Child of Achievement Award. I was so proud. We went to a very posh place in London and met lots of famous people and Brian May presented Andrew with his award. A few days later Radio Cornwall wanted him to give an interview. He agreed and I was really excited to hear his voice, so imagine how I felt when he didn't answer any of the questions but just chanted, "ooh arr Cantona", over and over again. Yes, you've guessed it! He was a BIG Manchester United fan and as both boys were mad about football he thought this was a cool thing to do. What could I say?

They had a lot of amazing outings. Andrew met Alex Ferguson and Martin had a VIP pass to watch Arsenal, the team he supported. Once, in London, they pretended to be Chelsea fans so they could look around the ground and changing rooms in order to "check out the opposition", they said.

Yes, they had a great time going to cricket matches, watching the rugby and enjoying all forms of sport. They probably did a lot more than most youngsters of their age. They had to, because time was not on their side. Of course, they weren't always swanning around the country. When they were at home they loved their PlayStation, watching DVDs and, most of all, listening to music – very, very loud music! It was a big part of their lives and their bedrooms looked like an HMV shop. I think they identified with a lot of the words in the songs.

The move to a secondary school without their friends was hard.

The local school was not adapted for wheelchairs. I was upset and worried for Andrew as he went off alone to Penair School in Truro. However, I need not have worried. He soon made friends with the son of his helper, who also had the condition. Martin followed a couple of years later and, although he didn't like school and I had to make him go, he was fine too.

Wanting to cram as much as possible into their lives I wrote to several charities to see what exciting experiences they could offer my boys. Within six months *Dreams Come True* replied and sent us to Florida with several other families whose children had life-limiting conditions, some the same as Andrew and Martin. We had the most fantastic time. They went everywhere and loved everything, particularly the funfair rides. Lifting them on and off was backbreaking, but they were living the life and that was all I cared about. I knew we might never have an opportunity like this again.

It wasn't all fun though, life never is. There were often difficult decisions to be made and I was the one who had to make them. I always listened to advice on what was the best thing to do to make the boys comfortable and live longer. There was an operation that would stop their backs from curving and make it easier for them to sit upright in their chairs. This would help prevent pressure on the heart and lungs, essential for their future health. Andrew was now fourteen and finally we decided to go for it. The night before the operation we arrived on the ward. As Andrew could do nothing for himself I was to stay with him. Imagine my horror when we ended up on the men's geriatric ward. There was no way I was going to stay there, so after a few choice words (you have to learn to be assertive) we were put into a side room. Just one problem, there was only one bed, and no room for anything else, so Andrew and I had to share. Andrew certainly wasn't happy about it and we didn't get much sleep, as you can imagine, but we did laugh about it in the end.

Andrew had his operation the next day. A massive eight hours in the theatre while I waited and worried. It was a huge shock to see him afterwards but, very slowly, he recovered and was able to go back home after a few weeks. He told me that the surgeons had stopped in the middle of his operation for a lunch break. Was he just winding me up? I never was sure. I was in awe at what he had undergone, two metal rods fused to his spine and he could still find something to laugh about. Martin underwent the same operation a few years later. It was so hard to see them have to have such a difficult procedure, but it made a huge difference to their lives and I never regretted my decision and they accepted it as part of what they had to undergo. They were both so brave and just got on with whatever life threw at them.

Fun came into their lives through the Tavistock Muscular Dystrophy Campaign, run entirely by volunteers, who raised funds to provide the youngsters with an annual holiday. They loved it and, over the years, made really good friends with both the other kids and the volunteer carers. Girls were an important part of these holidays, that and being away from Mum! Martin would have a new girlfriend every year, but Andrew had a special girl he thought the world of. I was told recently that she had called her baby boy after him. He would have loved that.

The boys took hundreds of photos while they were away. I have them still, and it's easy to see what a brilliant time they had. They went to places I have never been to and saw things I will never see. This was just what I wanted for them, to cram in as much as they could because time was not on their side.

After these holidays they were always low. They missed their friends and the freedom they were given and I wished I could have made everyday happy and exciting for them. However, it didn't last for long and with their incredible resilience they soon bounced back and became their usual mischievous selves.

The boys were a double act and this attracted everyone to them. They were very much the leaders of the gang and had their devoted followers who always kept in contact with them, and this helped us all through the hard times.

At the beginning of 1999 my marriage to the boys' dad broke up. It had really always been just the boys and me and so it did not affect them too much. Also at this time we were referred to Little Bridge House (LBH), the children's hospice. Oh my goodness, what a place. It was to change everything. I called it our little bit of heaven.

When you are a mum it is very hard to accept that anyone can look after your children as well as you do, but LBH completely changed my way of thinking. The boys were treated like kings and they loved it. They had the girls wrapped around their little fingers and the guys were all guys together, talking boy talk about sport, girls, drinking and, most important of all, what was for supper. Their wicked sense of humour soon made them very popular. I was able to make friends too and some of them, both parents and staff, will stay in my heart forever. Knowing the boys were cared for and happy I was able to relax and actually sleep undisturbed all night. What a treat!

As our stay came to an end we would always book the next one, trying to be there at the same time as our friends. I often wonder how the staff managed to cope with all the naughty boys being in the house at once, but they seemed not in the least fazed by their antics. One time, when two of their friends went out for the day, Andrew and Martin changed their rooms around completely, turning them pink and replacing their friends' names with girls' names. Finally, they filled them with soft toys and teddies in very rude positions. Everyone enjoyed the joke. No one ever denied them their bit of fun. Our stays at the hospice were always over too soon, but it was so reassuring to know they were always there in any kind of emergency.

We needed this support when Andrew had a really bad year. First he broke his leg, then his lung collapsed and after a long stay in hospital he still kept getting chest infections. At one point we really thought he was going to die. This was when the care team stepped in and LBH worked their magic and he made a remarkable recovery. Martin didn't escape without mishap either and in the following year fell out of the back of a bus. The driver had failed to deploy the lift and Martin, unable to see, just kept on moving his wheelchair backwards. He ended up with a broken arm and an injured head. Visiting him in the hospital later, and realising his injuries were fortunately not serious, I couldn't help laughing. With this huge bandage wrapped around his head he looked just like the Pope (now you know where the boys got their warped sense of humour from). Fortunately, once he'd looked in a mirror he saw the funny side of it too. After a few days in hospital he was off to LBH for tea and sympathy.

Both of them went on to college. Andrew took Media Studies and loved it, although, like all boys of that age, he was known to skip a few classes in favour of a trip to the shops and some retail therapy.

Martin and his friend Luke followed on a couple of years later.

I never did know what they were studying, unless girls were part of the curriculum! He always loved girls and once, without anyone knowing, drove all the way to the next village in his electric wheelchair to visit the latest girlfriend, not at all worried that he could have run out of charge and got stuck on some lonely country road. He was always up to something. I was once pushing him in his old wheelchair and he told me to stop as he was okay, he then went flying off down the hill, had a speed wobble and crashed into a stationary car. We made a very hasty escape I'm ashamed to say. They really were always getting into scrapes, because they would never let the fact that they were in a wheelchair hold them back. I lost count of the number of times they got stuck in mud, fell out or crashed.

There was never a dull moment at home. Friends forever passing through, cousins riding up and down the hall on the back of their chairs, lots of love and lots of noise. But isn't that how it should be with two teenagers in the house? And wasn't that what I had always wanted for my boys, a normal life?

We had been going to the hospice for over a year. It was a place where we felt at ease because everyone who went there was in the same situation. In spite of the fact that we faced the unthinkable no one was negative, there was no self-pity. I met so many brave parents and children who made me feel very humble. It was no wonder that none of us wanted to leave this place of kindness and understanding.

In 2000 we were privileged to take part in a TV programme about the hospice with a group of other parents. It was an exciting experience for the boys, who formed close bonds with the other children taking part. Sadly, only two of that group are still alive. But at the time it was all fun as the cameras whirled and the stars performed. One of the best bits was when they filmed Christmas early. The decorations were up, the festive food on the table and the presents under the tree. Brilliant! The very noisy carol service was however tinged with sadness and there were tears as we all realised this marked the end of the filming and we would be returning home, just the three of us once more. It had been wonderful to be with everyone and, although I had found talking about the boys difficult in front of the camera at times, being with other parents and building lasting friendships was worth it.

This had been a good year. The boys' health had stabilised and life was great. Andrew was to be eighteen and I arranged a surprise party for him with a strip-o-gram: was his face red! All his friends came and it was certainly a night to remember.

Two years later our lives changed again. We were staying at LBH and I went out with two of the other parents. During that evening I met my future husband Pete. Eventually we decided that this was it and the boys, our dog Badger and I left Cornwall and our friends for North Devon, to start a new life with Pete and his two sons, Ollie and Sam. Although my boys no longer went to college, their friends kept in touch and came to visit. Annual holiday continued and they were reunited with special friends. As young adults they moved on to Douglas House for their breaks where they met up with old mates from the LBH days. Here they indulged their love of live bands, even attending a concert by one of their favourites in Hyde Park.

The next few years were fairly good for us all. We operated well as a family group and Pete's younger boys got on famously with my two. But that was all to change.

In 2006, just after Andrew's twenty-third birthday, I noticed a change in him. I contacted LBH. Soon he was back in his 'home from home', being cared for by friends who knew him and his condition so well. I was greatly relieved as I think we all knew that he didn't have much longer to live. However, Andrew wasn't having any of that! He put up the biggest fight of his life and Pete and I never left his side, taking turns to sit with him. The staff saw to it that he had everything he needed or wanted – even cakes specially made by the cook. He was certainly given VIP treatment. The fight went on daily for seven months and during that time Pete and I decided to get married. We chose the date of my birthday and Martin gave me away. Dear Andrew was very ill but determined to be there and so, with both of my boys, family and friends present it was a very special day. As with everything my joy was tinged with sadness since Andrew had to return to Little Bridge immediately after the service.

One Sunday evening in May, two months after the wedding, he died peacefully, with all those who loved him so dearly gathered around him.

It was so sad to read the plans he had made for his own funeral, but in true Andrew fashion he had added his own inimitable humour. He wanted a particular dress code, the girls in short skirts and the boys in bad-taste T-shirts! He had chosen all the songs with lyrics that meant a lot to him. There were to be candles, balloons and fireworks to ensure he went out with a bang. Not wanting to be forgotten (as if that were possible), he wanted an Andrew Matthews Memorial Day.

He left such a gap in both my life and Martin's. He had crammed into an all too short life so many experiences and been loved by so many that he had certainly had a life worth living. Beneath the devilish humour there was kindness, consideration for others and bravery. These qualities made him a very special person.

Now the double act had ended and Martin was alone. He was very aware that he was destined to meet the same fate as his brother but showed remarkable resilience and somehow got on with his life. He was going to be twenty-one a few weeks after Andrew died and we went ahead with the planned party as we knew that was just what his brother would have wanted. It was a marvellous night, everyone came and we felt really supported by our friends. Andrew had made a card for Martin and we let off fireworks in his honour, so he was very much in all our thoughts.

Martin drank too much that night and this did become the pattern of his life for a while. I couldn't blame him, as it was his way of coping with his brother's death. He did, however, get into some hair-raising scrapes because of it, like the time he couldn't remember where he lived and only got home at all because someone, after several hours, finally recognised the trees leading up to the house. We got him into bed eventually, but after a few hours sleep he was up again, ready to party.

He made friends easily and he was always accepted as one of the gang. The fact that the house a friend lived in was at the top of a steep flight of steps, proved no barrier at all if invited to a party. The boys simply rolled up their sleeves and carried him and his wheelchair up to the top, no problem.

He still went to Douglas House a few times a year where he and his mates, now young adults, got up to all kinds of mischief. I remember one occasion when he told me they had all gone to a strip club and enjoyed a private strip. That was Martin, ever one of the boys. Another time he informed Pete and I and Laura, his carer, that he had arranged for a prostitute to come to the house. This set off a huge argument and in the end I walked out and left them to it. Later that day I got a call from Pete to say that Martin had changed his mind. Relief all round, but he certainly had us going there for a while.

Martin loved company, lots of it. Whether it was family, friends or the doggy variety. He had two labradoodles, George and Ruby, who were devoted to him. As a puppy George would sleep under his wheelchair. They would do anything for him and would always wake him up by jumping on his bed and licking him until he could hardly breathe.

He was always full of energy and up to something and people loved him because of his spirit and obvious enjoyment of life. Sam and Ollie, like the dogs, would do anything for him, even letting him use their fingers to play on the X Box when his weren't working very well. They loved his sense of fun. One New Year's Eve he went out dressed as a chicken. He looked so good he scared the dogs half to death, but all his friends thought it was great.

Martin really did enjoy his life the best he could, and I'm glad that he did. I now realise that Andrew's and Martin's need for people, noise and laughter was to block out what was going to happen to them. There was no future for these boys so they had to make the very most of the present. They knew that and got on with what life had to offer them. They lived for now. This wasn't selfish because it helped me, and those who loved them, to cope too. We really did laugh about most things and on bad days we muddled through and when they were over we'd breathe a sigh of relief and smile again. It must have taken great courage on their part to be so positive in the face of such adversity.

Unlike his brother, Martin died suddenly in 2010, three years and four months after Andrew's death. He was twenty-four. I had now lost both my boys, my only children, to muscular dystrophy.

It is hard to end this story because really there is no end. Andrew and Martin are still here, an essential part of me, in my heart and in my head. I think about them every second of every day and wish we could have just one more word, one more moment, one more hug. They have left a huge gap in my life and sometimes I cry, but often, I laugh. Writing this has given me the opportunity to think back and remember the mad, crazy antics they both got up to and how, because of who they were, they have left me not just tears but laughter. When they were alive I took photos of them in my mind, and they will be there until the day I die. I know that for as long as I live I will remember something to make me smile each day – that is their lasting gift to me. They both had to face the unthinkable and they did it with courage and humour and I am very proud to be their mum. They were, and are, my inspiration to carry on.

The Boys by their Grandfather

As their Grandad I felt a mixture of shock and horror when their terrible illness was diagnosed. The shock to my daughter when she came out of the doctor's room meant she could not speak; she just cried uncontrollably. I had to go in myself to find out what was going on and was told that Andrew had the worst case of muscular dystrophy the doctor had ever come across in a boy so young. When I asked him what we could do he simply said, "Go home and prepare for the worst."

It took ages to find out more about the condition and then we found that Martin had the same terrible thing. Had my daughter been tested at the time of Andrew's birth then Martin may have been spared. So Nicola had to go through the heartache and stress again. When I found out that it was a genetic condition passed on to my daughter from me and her mother, well, that brought on self-blame, which took some years to fade. As the boys were growing up they were full of fun. I remember playing on their computer games with them and them telling me how useless I was. They were so full of life and normal, but whatever fun we had together, for me it was always tinged with sadness that I would never be able to take them out on the boat or have a game of football with them. But those boys, in spite of everything, lived life to the full. I thank all the people who gave time and money to give them the experiences and trips they so enjoyed. They did everything. I wasn't sure what to make of them going to a strip club mind – I've never been to one myself, but that's teenagers today I suppose.

Now all my hopes are for my daughter that, having given so much to her boys, she can now give herself a life. We all miss those boys so much but now it's got to be her time to enjoy her life.

Words from Pete, stepfather to Andrew and Martin

Since meeting Nicola and her boys I have seen life for what it really is, fun and laughter mixed in with sadness and pain. For me it was a very different life from the one I had led before, but one that welcomed me and my sons in and gave us all something very special. We will never forget Andrew and Martin. There was a lesson for us all in the way they dealt with their illness, never letting it get the better of them, so determined were they in every way to fully live their lives.

I hope to meet them both again one day!

Heather
By Alison

Andy and I lost our princess in 2011 and, to be honest, I am still raw with sadness. Why wouldn't I be? But I think my incredible daughter deserves her story to be told, so here goes. You'll have to forgive me if, sometimes, I wander off track.

The path of my life was not what I would necessarily have chosen. It forced me along an often difficult and testing road, but there were joyous times when the way seemed straight, clear and full of promise. The births of my children were two such times. In 1981 my son Michael was born, two weeks early. Then in 1984 Heather arrived in an even greater rush, eight weeks before she was expected! I was taken into hospital for emergency surgery. The doctors all thought a tiny premature baby would emerge, but instead, to their amazement a chubby 7lb 1oz girl was born.

She was Heather as soon as I saw her, but the immense joy I felt at her birth was very soon replaced with acute anxiety when, an hour later, she became very ill. The battle had begun.

With underdeveloped vital organs, her lungs could not cope with her size and so began the long struggle for life. Heather fought like a lion, urged on every day by me, begging her to keep going so that we could go home where she belonged, but it was some months before we could be discharged. Her weight fluctuated dramatically, at one point dipping down to just two pounds, and it was not until she had stabilised that the long-awaited day finally came.

H, as we called her, was a delight, a happy and contented baby and, of course, much loved. She did have problems related to her birth and would sometimes forget to breathe, so she certainly kept us on our toes. She could be very mischievous and sometimes would hold her breath deliberately, turn blue and then burst out laughing at the general panic she had caused. We spent an awful lot of those early months in hospital clinics, but were fortunate to have a wonderful consultant. Heather loved him and he always called her poppet, throughout all the years he looked after her.

Whatever we needed to do we did, happy in the knowledge that it was a small price to pay for what we had, a complete family. However, when H was 18 months I became concerned by her lack of development and she didn't seem to want to crawl. I was told not to worry by my doctor but I still felt enough concern to take her off, under my own steam, to Great Ormond Street. I hoped they would see me as a fussy mum and send me on my way but, deep down, I knew there was something wrong, and sadly I was right. A scan revealed ventilation damage to the side of her brain dealing with motor skills, which meant H was unlikely to either walk or talk.

So that was that. I scooped her up in my arms, collected Mathew from the hospital school, and we caught the train back to Plymouth. Heather sat on my knees smiling at everyone around her and they smiled back, making friendly comments on my lovely family. Only I knew that my life had changed forever.

Unable to cope with the prospect of such an upheaval in his life, my husband eventually left, and H never saw him again. For the next five years, with no family support and very much alone, all I wanted was for both my children to be okay. So I worked night shifts in order to be there during the day for H, at her special needs playgroup, and for Michael at school. During any spare time I had – in between shopping, washing and cooking – you would find my head in a book trying to find a new treatment for H. Somehow, I managed on very little sleep.

About this time I heard of a clinic in Budapest that offered a treatment called Conductive Education. It involved re-teaching the good side of the brain to do what the other side could no longer do. I was interested but, and it was a big but, it was very expensive. They only had six places for English children who might benefit and, if we were suitable, we'd have to stay there for six months. It seemed very daunting, but if it would give H the chance to walk I had to go for it.

After three long months we got the letter. We were accepted! So, with the money raised and Michael's homework sorted, the three of us were off.

I always wanted to give both my children the best start in life but at this moment it was H who needed more help than Michael. I did find it scary being on my own and having to make these decisions. Another worry was that I would be expected to become an expert in conductive therapy, as work would have to continue when we returned home. I would have to learn the repeat and do technique.

In reality, all these fears were unfounded. My A-star girl thrived on the work and every goal she passed made her so proud of herself. Within a year she was walking with the aid of a chair and then with her own customised walker. My heart sang. I felt that all the tears and heartache had been worth it and that I had made the right decision. But I was soon to be tested in my belief.

In spite of H rejoicing in her walking I was aware that it was creating pressure on her hips and eventually they dislocated.

Although not in pain, she soon became uncomfortable and I began to doubt myself. Was I really doing the best thing for her? Major surgery was the only answer if she was to continue walking. I had terrible feelings of guilt for putting her through such pain. But H bounced back after the operation, recovered well and was soon back at school using her walker. Little did I know that there were many more battles ahead. But first …

In December 1991, something wonderful happened to us, so unexpected and fortunate in every way. A lovely man who lived down our street stepped into our lives. The children were nine and six. Michael had a new football buddy. And H? Well, she had a man she could wrap around her finger. It was love at first sight and she chose him to be the only dad she would ever know. Andy didn't stand a chance.

Looking back, I had a clear view of the road then. It spread out before us, wide and straight, leading us all the way into a new house where we could live as a real family again.

As H became more dependent, our lives began to revolve around her timetable. We tried hard to help her continue to walk independently, but a second hip operation left her in a full body cast for twelve weeks. During this time Andy manfully pushed the enormous chair, puffing and panting as he went, with H giggling at his efforts. But once she was out of plaster we didn't feel it was right to risk damaging her hips again, so H ended up in a wheelchair. I found this very hard. I felt sad, but H did what she always did, she smiled and got on with it, and I felt ashamed for feeling sorry for myself.

What I found most exhausting was being a grown-up, having to make the decisions that would map out another human being's life. There was often a feeling of isolation too. I found that friends become fewer and more distant when you have a special child. Perhaps they think you may expect something from them, when really all you want is that they stay your friend and be the same as before.

We were, however, a close unit and life for the four of us went on. Although we often felt like square pegs in round holes, our love was strong and kept us going as we slipped into a definite routine. We loved walking in the countryside, often to quite inaccessible places where the wheelchair couldn't go. But Andy devised a way of using a back carrier. In bright green and yellow, H loved being carried on her dad's back, particularly over the hills. "Just don't eat any more of that chocolate or I'll never get you up the next hill!" Andy would shout back over his shoulder. H would throw back her head, roar with laughter and take another bite. Andy often reminds me of these happy times.

We didn't ever see H's disability, although we were very much aware of it. It did not define her and so if other people were negative towards her I found it very hurtful. But H smiled her way through life, shaming those who rudely stared and melting the hearts of those who chose to give her a second look as they passed by.

In 1995 we faced another crisis. After a severe chest infection H deteriorated so quickly that she was rushed into intensive care and put on a ventilator, fighting for her life. During the difficult weeks of treatment that followed we camped out in her room, keeping constant watch. Eventually, we were told arrangements were being made for our return home as H was not expected to survive long without the ventilator and surgery was not an option since, even if she survived, the care she would require would totally destroy the quality of all our lives.

It took some time for us to convince the doctors that if there was any chance of saving Heather's life we wanted them to go ahead. We would deal with the aftermath in our own way. We had travelled difficult roads before and were familiar with the territory, all that mattered was that H travelled with us. The surgeon finally agreed but stressed that we would probably only have two years with H after the operation – to us, a lifetime of living – then he went on to list everything H would not be able to do:

- no eating (feeding tube)

- no drinking

- no swimming

- no baths

- no showers (bed baths only)

- no school …

We just nodded as the list continued and, when he'd finished, asked him to get on with it.

Our girl came home six weeks later. With her came a mini-hospital of drugs and equipment. We'd been given our instructions before we left the hospital as to what H could not do. I remember looking the surgeon in the eye and fervently promising to do all in my power to care for her and protect her, and also telling him that he must understand that she had fought to live and LIVE she would, if we had anything to do with it.

H was smiling; our family was whole again and we felt we could cope with anything. In reality it proved to be hard on many levels. For one thing, H had forgotten how to sleep – the result of a medical coma when the body loses its sense of natural time – so she and I survived on ten-minute naps. We had problems with her tracheotomy, her nasal feed, all manner of things connected to her medical and everyday care. But we had chosen to do it ourselves without any help, and do it we would. Andy worked part time, but we relied totally on each other and, as a strong team, we managed. H enjoyed life and accepted certain limitations with her usual smile. She rarely complained, never showing the sadness I sometimes could not hide.

Then in 1998 we were introduced to the hospice. As soon as we got there we recognised we were in a protected place that would become our sanctuary. This was where we found true friends who understood. In the end they were to become our second family, one we could always rely on.

The allotted two years came and went and H thrived. She now went to a special school where a friendly nurse attended to her medical needs, and she loved it. She went swimming, enjoyed the trampoline, often turning blue with laughter and, with the dreaded list behind her, life was good. She was always pleased to see me when I collected her and we would settle onto the sofa and watch TV. This was our time for treats. H now had a peg, which meant that she could chew and swallow a little, though there was a risk of chest infection. But infections were always going to be part of her life and we had decided long ago that she was not going to live in a bubble but enjoy her life.

When Andy came home she instantly became daddy's girl and I would leave them watching football with a bowl of crisps and a bottle of Guinness, which she loved. Each happy and contented in the other's company.

Unfortunately, in 2007 Heather's health began to deteriorate and she was confined to home. She also tended to sleep more because of the heavy medication she was given to make her comfortable. Too old now for the children's hospice, we found ourselves alone once again. As always, we relied on each other, spending our time with H, listening to her music, watching her favourite films and programmes and, if the weather was good, sitting on the balcony looking out at her beloved garden.

In 2011 she developed pneumonia. I was sure she would be okay as I had seen her ill so many times and she had always pulled through. But her body was too tired and this time she lost the battle.

We lay with her until dawn. She looked so beautiful, as if she was just asleep. The doctor came early that morning, confirmed her death and said there was no need for her to leave home. He put us in touch with Rupert, a Funeral Director. He was a lovely man (H would have picked him herself) and helped us take care of her in her own home, as we had always done. We never left her alone, although people started arriving at the house. Where had they been when H was alive?

The following days passed in a blur. Snow and ice caused all funerals to be cancelled. Heather was at home for fifteen days. The funeral came and went. I remember the wild flowers, the white horses, Trouble and Strife, the service. Only snippets.

Thinking over our busy life caring for H I ask myself: was I selfish? Should I have given up? The truth is I couldn't, not when she was fighting so hard to live. Heather survived twelve years longer than the doctors predicted and I believe it was because she enjoyed her life and knew we adored her. We let her do everything she was capable of doing. We never allowed her illness or disability to hold her back.

Then what? Well, three months later Andy and I found ourselves treading a very different, quite unexpected path. We were to embark on an African Adventure and Heather was the reason.

It all began when, after weeks of numbing sadness, I woke very early one morning. It was still dark and I could see by the clock it was just after 4am. I knew this day was going to be different, I felt clear-headed at last and knew what I wanted to do. I woke Andy and told him, "I want to go to Africa." Even in his dazed state he realised I was serious. Over our morning coffee I explained that I wanted to take all Heather's belongings and give them to those children who really needed help. Andy had his doubts. We'd only ever travelled as far as Disneyland Paris and I had a serious heart condition, which left me very unwell at times. But he could tell that, for the first time since losing H, I wanted to do more than stay in bed. He knew it was important to me.

During his lunch break that very day he worked his magic on the computer and returned in the evening with all the information we needed. He had tracked down a village in Kenya and contacted the Elder, Du, who gave permission for us to go and give the poor and orphaned children the support and help they so badly needed. It was now up to us to make it happen.

There was a huge amount of planning to do. Jabs, insurance (mine was a fortune), visas and plane connections. All very testing when you are not seasoned travellers. We were going to pay the chief to give us safe travel from Nairobi to his village as the journey could be dangerous for white people and would take over five hours by road. We also arranged to stay with a local family who would introduce us to everyone. So it was all agreed and there was no turning back.

On 10th April H's school was placing a memorial stone in their garden. At the get-together afterwards we told everyone our plans. Many of them, including the Headmaster, thought we were mad and felt it was unsafe to venture alone into what everyone knew was a trouble spot. But, seeing our minds were made up, they were very much behind us and started collecting anything and everything they thought the children would find useful.

At 6.30am on 14th June we left our home for Kenya, East Africa, in memory of our very special daughter. We had a long day ahead of us and were nervous but excited. The eight cases we brought with us were waved through at Cairo, but we were not so lucky with the Kenyan authorities, who made us pay excess baggage. The flight was crowded and very hot, after a while it became smelly too – I don't suppose deodorant is high on their list of priorities. Later it became very cold and we were given blankets. Although Andy managed to sleep I was too scared to nod off. At 4am we arrived in Nairobi, nearly 24 hours after we'd set off. The airport was huge, armed guards patrolled everywhere and it was so quiet I felt very vulnerable in this sea of black faces. However, there was a welcoming smile from the customs man as he waved us through. Outside the Airport was buzzing with noise and activity. We were besieged by people and within five minutes were surrounded by faces and voices, some wanting to drive us out of the airport, others trying credit card scams, and many begging for money. We were so relieved when a man shouted our name and we realised it was James, our contact, picking us up in the family van, as arranged.

The journey took six hours. Andy slept in the back. I sat next to James, following the road, over tarmac and rubble, through remote villages and townships. The heat and dry dust filled the air. I smelt fire-cooked food. I spied derelict wooden buildings with women and *hoochies* (drunks) moving about; it looked like some were dancing and I could hear lively music, which made me smile. I had never seen darkness so black and the only light on the road was from our dim headlights. We drove with all the windows closed as James explained that white people were often targets for bandits and it was unsafe anywhere after dark. I prayed we didn't break down. There were groups of men and woman walking along in the darkness, children too, strung out in aimless lines along the edge of the road. As the van slowly passed by they would peer in through the windows, showing only the whites of their eyes. James said that most crimes were committed on these roads and that everyone carried knives, machetes and batons. I was terrified. Stretched out in the back, Andy slept on, totally unaware.

Suddenly, the sky opened up as if someone had zipped back the cover and dawn broke. The sun was warm, even though it was winter, and we were there at last. Waiting at the village was a welcoming party, led by the biggest man I have ever seen. When he smiled his fierce expression changed and his whole face lit up. This was Joseph and he was to sleep near us at night. We were to be given the protection of the family and no one messed with his family. They owned most of the land and people relied on them for work. They also dealt with their own problems, gave out their own punishments and were a law unto themselves. So we were safe.

In the quiet of our hut, we listened to the birds and insects and recovered from our journey before exploring the village. It was a mixture of wooden and brick buildings (*shambas*) and it was obvious which belonged to the chief and his family. We were to learn that, even here, there was a clear divide between poor and poorer.

We met Lucy, the eldest daughter, who was a striking woman, sitting outside her *shamba*. She, like all the older women, spoke very little English since she had not learnt it at school. But there was an immediate connection between us. Andy insisted on chopping up a large tree for her (woman's work!) and within no time produced a pile of logs. This brought a huge smile to her face and he was her favourite from then on.

The first few days we spent settling in to the routine of village life. I helped the women with their chores but Andy would not let me do the backbreaking work of planting crops as it was so hot and he felt I would struggle because of my heart. We did whatever we could and were soon accepted by everyone, and believe me, some of them were hard to please! There was very little food to be had as the crops had failed through lack of rain. So we were pleased that we were contributing money that would help the whole village, who relied on milk cow money to keep them going.

The day finally came when we could visit the school. I couldn't wait to get there. We had decided to walk the five kilometres because we wanted to get used to the route we would be travelling every day. After Lucy's flour pancakes and a banana, we were given instructions on how to keep ourselves safe. Basically shout out, "we're staying with the family". We set off.

As we walked along the track on the hard compacted soil, meeting only the odd donkey or cow searching for grass, I thought about how far we had come and how this new road was taking us towards a fresh challenge, undertaken in Heather's name. As we neared the school we came on a local market. Villagers were selling their meagre crops and children, some as young as five, ran about brandishing their machetes. No school for them. Everyone seemed to carry something for protection as they walked the deserted, dangerous roads for water or wood.

We were a curiosity and the centre of much attention. As we entered the wooden gate, the schoolchildren literally stopped in their tracks. Then they started waving and shouting, 'jambo'. Inside, we were given a cup of milky tea, a mixture of milk, water and sugar beet given to the children each day to keep them full. They receive no other food during the day. There were 350 pupils and each child received £10 a year from the government. This was for their education and to pay the teachers' wages. No money was provided for the special needs children and they were simply in the building to keep them safe. My job was to assess these children, using my Constructive Education training, and write a report on each one to try to get the government to provide funding. I was also going to instruct a young teacher in these methods so that he could carry on the work when we left. Andy was going to buy paint and decorate the dark, drab classrooms with the help of the enthusiastic pupils. Ironically, the only colours available were blue and yellow, used on all official government buildings and sold by the government store. But that was fine! Our plans were set and we had one month to make a difference.

The work at the school was everything we could have hoped for and more. At first, we were quite an attraction. Andy always had a crowd watching him at break times. Then they got used to our faces and we became part of their day. I assessed all thirteen special needs children in fifteen days, the young teacher beside me making notes. He was amazed at what they could do and, after a shaky start, we became great pals. All the children could be helped in some basic way. There was Lewis, 14 years old and with cerebral palsy, who had been put out on the streets at six years old and had received no education, even though the school had taken him in. I soon realised that he understood numbers and within a day could count up to ten. He went on to knowing his name and how to write it, then being able to say and write the alphabet. He was so proud of himself and, given time, would be able to learn the skills that would enable him to work on a farm rather than be left begging on the streets. He teamed up with another boy, Ian, who had spent his time at the school peeping through doors. Once he was given a chance to learn English he and Lewis would sit together and 'chat', something they had never done before. They became great mates and, with the continued help of the staff, they could both have a chance at a better future.

Andy and I were aware of the pride of these people and wanted to spend time at the school really getting to know them. The staff helped identify the very needy families and we began the painful task of distributing H's clothes and belongings. When we see Africa on television, with celebrities visiting poor villages, it often looks grim. Believe me, the reality is very sobering, their everyday lives are so difficult. These people do suffer, feeling pain and hunger much of the time but, in spite of this, what they do a lot of is SMILE. They gave me hope for the future, and I began to think that Andy and I would, eventually, really smile again.

When we walked home from school the children would walk with us as far as they had to go. We would listen to them singing their songs and we would try to join in, which would set them off laughing. We enjoyed those walks because everyone now greeted us with a smile and a wave. We were living among them and ate and slept like them, so they accepted us into their community.

'Without' for us is not having our daughter, but we do not have the added burden of being without basic needs, like the people we had come to know. They too experience the loss of their children, or a close family member, but they also have to go without water, food, warmth, often on a daily basis. They don't have the stuff we all work for and crave and yet there is a spirit inside them that keeps them looking forward and makes them believe that one day everything will all be okay. When we lost H the stuff we had worked hard for and treasured meant nothing to us any more. We had not known 'without' until then.

We had no choice here but to live without stuff and somehow it gave Andy and I a chance to breathe. Without things we felt released. This simple life, far away from all we had ever known gave us freedom and we loved every day.

After three weeks of getting to know the needs of the poorest families we started to put bags together for them. H had a lot of clothes and shoes and we were actually able to supply twenty families and give thirty children some kind of footwear. The boys weren't bothered about what colour the jumpers or boots were, pink was fine with them. The most prized outfit was a Chelsea and England football kit. I gave it to a young widowed mother of two boys. She cried when she opened the bag and told us it was the dream of her sons to own such a kit. Two days later she walked the four miles to school to give us a handwritten letter of thanks from her boys and a beaded necklace she had made for me. I treasure them both.

It was not long before the children began to appear at school in their 'new' clothes. It was hard to see them dressed in Heather's clothes but they were all so excited and proud that I knew H would have been delighted and that, given the chance, this was something she would have done herself, for my girl had an angel's soul.

We also managed to help a widowed mother, Marion. Her eldest son was twenty and worked as a guide for the family. She also had Cruga, who was eight, and two young girls. They were a lovely family but very, very poor. And yet, the first time we met her she cooked a meal for us. I really cannot describe how bad her *shamba* was. The only light came from the open wooden door. The walls were covered in cardboard to try to keep in some heat and there was a rough, mud floor. The whole family lived in one tiny room. We spent a couple of hours with them, sharing the little they had and they were a joy to be with. The boys spoke some English so it was easy for Marion to relate to us. They were so pleased when we gave the last bundle of clothes to the girls and Cruga a pair of H's blue Doc Martens. The boots were covered in a pattern of white daisies but he didn't seem to mind. In fact, he fell in love with them, immediately put them on and began strutting around in them. James smiled and told us they would be worn until Cruga could no longer squeeze his feet into them and then they would be passed on to the girls.

Before we left, I gave Marion all my clothes and we took a photograph of them all, dressed up and smiling. We didn't forget Lucy and her sisters who were always cold at night, so we gave them H's scarves and woolly bobble hats to wear in bed.

I managed to finish all the reports before we left on the last Friday of our stay. We were given two bags of African tea so I could make milky tea, when I got home. The staff put on a lovely meal in our honour, only spoilt by the hungry pupils peering enviously through the doorway. I was not allowed to share my food with any of them because, as the Headmaster said, if they hadn't enough money to feed all the children then they would feed none.

On our last weekend, Andy and I set out on a twelve-mile walk to the foot of Mount Kenya. This was the real Africa, miles along cracked, mud roads in searing heat, women in the fields, slaving away on the land trying to encourage weak crops to grow. Suddenly, just 200 yards from all this poverty and hardship, stood a luxurious five star hotel; bright green lawns constantly refreshed by sprinklers gushing precious water, a profusion of exotic flowers and rich, white guests enjoying the best of what was on offer. It was really disturbing to come across such a stark contrast.

We did complete the walk (with a lot of help from Andy towards the end to keep me going) and were rewarded by the sight of a troop of colobus monkeys swinging in the trees above. It was a truly beautiful place and I was so pleased we had made the effort to go.

The final few days sped past, Sunday church with Lucy, the congregation clapping and singing at the tops of their voices, and me doing my best to join in. Then the final treat, a day's safari. Lucy rarely left the village and so we took her along with us. Here was wildlife in its natural habitat: buffalo, wild boar, giraffe and elephant right in front of us and, deep in the trees and hidden from sight, a lioness with her young, alert and listening to our jeep and warning us off with her roars.

The following day Lucy and I went for some last minute shopping to the market in a dusty, dirty town. It was a fascinating but violent place where fighting could break out over the least little thing. Lucy told me, to my horror, that the day before a man had been hacked to death for trying to cheat a stallholder by underpaying for his bread! We found the pots and pans I wanted and hurried away past the meat stalls – with unfamiliar carcasses hanging in the sun, covered in flies – and through the crowds of colourful sellers trying to persuade us to buy their wares. It was a strange experience, in one way exciting but in another very scary. Perhaps sometimes you need to be scared to feel alive.

The day for our final goodbyes had come and we had bought 800 biscuits as a treat for the children. The family had given us a shrub for H and Lewis and Ian, delighted to be the ones chosen, planted it in the schoolyard. Andy received an award for painting the school and me for my work with the children. Then we were asked to present a prize to the Outstanding Pupil of the Month. It was only a pencil but you would have thought it was made of solid gold, the boy who received it was so excited. The final, and for us the most touching part of the occasion, was when we were shown a sign that had been fixed above the newly-created special needs classroom. It read, In Memory of Heather Alison Kebby.

It felt sad saying goodbye, but we had done what we came to do and made some wonderful friends. It was time to go.

As we drove to the Airport, the sight of an old man driving an ancient moped down the road made me smile. He had the back stacked with old Cola crates, Andy counted 16, and the bike wobbled all over the place, while the old boy smoked his baccy, totally unconcerned by traffic narrowly missing him as it passed.

On the long flight home I thought about Africa, the places we had seen and the people we had met. I remembered the faces of woman washing their clothes by the river and their look of amazement when, by adding a little of the detergent I had brought with me, the dirt and dust ran out into the water with no effort at all. And I thought of our good friend Lucy. She had taught me to cook her way and she had made us many lovely meals, seemingly out of nothing.

Then I remembered one incident when her food was not so good! She was worried I was not eating enough and had asked Andy what my favourite food was. He had replied chicken. As I sat by the fire, drinking tea and cutting up vegetables for supper I became aware of a very bad smell coming from the bubbling pot. I asked Lucy what it was and she proudly announced that we were having chicken for supper. The liquid in the pot was thick and grey. She explained that, after plucking, they chop up the whole bird and boil it for several hours to kill any disease it may have. Normally these scrawny hens were only kept for eggs. I knew how precious they were and how very kind and generous it was of her to do this for me, but I can't describe how bad that meal was. Not wishing to offend her I waited until she was busy and slipped my share to the child next to me, who grinned and got stuck in. Lucy's mother had the head and beak and spent the rest of the evening sucking on it, the other women shared the bones and the children had the stock. The meat, what there was of it, was reserved for the men.

I looked across at Andy fast asleep in the seat next to me. He was such a star when it came to food, he would always eat whatever was put in front of him, no questions asked, and Lucy had loved him for it. With pictures of our African adventure swirling around in my head I too, eventually, fell asleep.

We walked back into our house on the 16th of July, six months after we lost Heather. Home no longer felt like home, it was cold and empty and the silence made me panic. I put the empty suitcases away the next day, the last of my girl's things had gone and her beloved room was empty, I hoped she did not think I was trying to forget her. After all, it was in her memory we had made the trip and taken risks with our own lives in order to celebrate hers. I'd been a long way away from medical help, but apart from the heat and feeling tired, I'd kept really well, and didn't need treatment until I returned. I would like to think that Heather looked after me and allowed me to do what I had set out to do. We knew she would love it that a little girl in Africa loved wearing her pink top, as much as she had! I knew she would approve of all those happy, smiling faces. It was because of her that we were able to make a difference to so many other young people's lives.

At twenty-five my life changed and Heather filled my days. There were times when it was hard, but it was our 'normal' and she taught us such a lot about love and acceptance that any other life would have meant a different H, and we would not have changed her for the world. It was because of her that Andy and I had our amazing adventure and it is heartening to know that my wonderful girl is remembered in a far off land by people she never knew but who give thanks for her life.

P.S. When you next meet a disabled child smile and say hello, for you are in the presence of a very special person.

A memorial in a remote village in Kenya

Kimberley

By Julia

Darren and I had been together for eight years, married for seven, before we decided to try for a baby. Eighteen months later Kimberley Nicole Office arrived at the grand weight of 5lb 4oz. We couldn't have been more thrilled.

During our married life Darren and I had pretty much spent our time much to ourselves. Yes, we had close friends and were sociable, but on the whole we were very private people.

For the first six weeks of Kimberley's life, we were like any other new parent — tired, unsure, learning as each day arrived, but also feeling so proud.

The day of Kimbers' six week check up was to be the beginning of so many unwanted bombshells that we would hear through the next seventeen years. Looking back though we managed to take them on the chin and rose to the challenge. We never let any bad news get us down too much. Our lives changed completely with various professionals coming and going, hospital appointments and visits. Darren had to take a lot of time off and we needed some financial help, and that meant more meetings and more people. It seemed as if our life was theirs and Darren and I often remarked on how once we had been quite private people but not anymore!

But we got on with it for Kimbers and we miss it terribly because she is no longer here.

I had wanted to write about Kimberley and her life many years ago, but something held me back. Was it because it would be there in black and white? Would that make it more real? Was it that Kimberley might find it and read the brutal truth that she wouldn't reach adulthood? I wanted to protect her from that. No child should have to live with that knowledge. How little we knew.

Now I can write in memory of you, Kimberley.

When I was asked to write about our daughter, of whom we are so proud, I felt filled with dread that I would let Kimberley down. I worried that it would open up such a torrent of emotions that I wouldn't be able to control them. But I felt I owed it to Kimbers. I know that she will never be forgotten, but she won't always be remembered as we remember her now and, by having a small part of her life written down in this book, her legacy will live on forever.

People on the 'outside' often mentioned how amazing we were as a family and how courageous and brave Kimbers was. It's funny how people see your life from a different angle. We led it normally and didn't really consider ourselves particularly different from other families; neither were we concerned about what others thought. We all just got on with living.

Kimberley's life-limiting illness never defined who she was and it didn't drive us as a family. Nor do I think her condition made Kimbers a stronger person, she was strong in the first place. I believe this came in part from the fact that we treated her as we did our other children. We faced the hurdles facing Kimberley (and there were many) as best we could, and then moved on. We didn't dwell on the illness, or the problems that came our way because of it, but constantly looked ahead, trying to be positive, however difficult it was. We never let her think it was so bad that she, or any of the family, couldn't enjoy life. She was brought up to feel that her condition was part and parcel of her life and she responded with resilience, courage and, most of all, humour. We didn't keep her wrapped in cotton wool; if she wanted to try something, we let her, obviously within reason! As a teenager she wanted to do what her peers did and, naturally, this included going into town on her own and hanging out with her friends. We let her go, but I must admit we spent many an anxious time clock watching until she returned.

We always told her how proud we were of her and she typically brushed this aside as if what she coped with was perfectly normal, that it was no big deal. She would question us sometimes as to why we had to tell people about the medicines, the needles, the oxygen, the hospital appointments, the pain, and the operations. Why was it necessary? She never thought of herself as ill and never wanted a fuss. In primary school someone mentioned about her being ill, she replied, "Me? I'm not ill."

Kimberley was on oxygen from an early age and took it for granted. When she started at secondary school, someone once asked her why she was on it. Kimbers had no idea and came home and said, "I felt a bit stupid as I didn't know!" and laughed.

As parents we did the 'normal' stuff: we complained about the state of her bedroom; that her music was too loud; argued about the time she should go to bed; told her off because she hadn't put enough effort into her homework; the usual living with a teenager list. Just because the prognosis wasn't good didn't mean we allowed her to shirk anything. We still maintained boundaries.

Kimbers had regular hospital appointments, which she loved as it meant a day off school, a lie-in and, generally, lunch out. After these appointments we would always ask her if she had any questions, or if there was anything the consultant had said that she didn't understand. She would regularly reply, "No, not really." She wasn't bothered and thought it was all rather boring, which she actually once said. There were more important things for her to think about, like getting back on Facebook and texting her friends.

I have fond memories, among the very sad ones, of these times. Strange as it might sound Kimberley, her daddy and myself would have such fun at these appointments. We always had lots of laughs people-watching and joking around while we waited outside each department for various tests. The staff knew Kimbers and she had a good rapport with them, chatting about school, the movies, or what takeaway she would be having on the way home. Yes, we found joy in the most unexpected places.

I'm not saying life was easy. There were days when she was unwell and in pain, but she never complained. You could always get a smile or a giggle out of her. She'd take her medication, have a massage – any excuse – and carry on. Some days were worse than others but, as soon as she was feeling better, we'd always send her off to school. There were times I felt a bit hard, but you aim for a normal life, you don't do things just in case something awful happens or because the future is uncertain. You carry on.

We never thought that Kimberley would actually die. She had got over so many major illnesses, some of which involved long spells in hospital, some in the intensive care unit, but she always managed to pull through. She always came home.

One of the hardest things I ever had to do was talk to her about her funeral. Can you imagine ever having such a conversation with your child?

Apparently, Kimbers had spoken to a carer at Little Bridge House, our wonderful children's hospice, about wanting to talk to us about her funeral. She didn't want to bring it up in case she upset us! Can you believe it? Her main concern was to spare us.

Children have such a gift of compartmentalising things in their lives. It is staggering to think they are capable of talking about, and planning, what they want when they die, and then carrying on with the normal everyday things in their lives. It took my breath away to know that our 16-year-old daughter could plan her own funeral and then carry on with life. We felt humbled by her sheer bravery.

I understand now that planning the funeral doesn't mean that you're chancing fate, or that you're accepting that it is going to happen. If you are honest with yourself you know it will happen, sooner than you want, but you have to live with that knowledge. Many people fear that if you're discussing it, you are making it more real and perhaps making it come sooner. Others take the opposite view and think that by not focusing on it, it makes the inevitable disappear, almost. With hindsight I realise neither of these is true.

Our wish was to make sure that we knew exactly what Kimbers wanted and had planned. Boy, did she have stuff planned! We hoped to set her mind at rest by assuring her that her wishes would be fulfilled. I was aware that for her dad, her brothers and me it would be one of the worst days of our lives. However, we didn't want to regret that we had got it wrong by missing something vital out. Planning gives you time to get it right and, after all, that is so important as it is the last thing you can do for your child. One of the requests Kimberley had was that she could go to Little Bridge House when she died. I needed to help her understand that if she died at home this would not be possible; however, everything else was.

The day we discussed all this seems so surreal now. Kimberley had come back from LBH with a letter containing her request for her funeral. I remember she kept following me around with it in her hand. I kept saying "in a minute", as I really didn't want to read it. Eventually, I knew that I had to because it was what she wanted and if she was brave enough to write this letter and discuss it then I had to be big enough to face it too.

We sat on the bed in her room to read it together. The phone kept ringing and people kept knocking on the front door. In the end they were so persistent I had to answer it. I could have done without those interruptions right in the middle of this awful part of our lives but, with Kimber's help, we just laughed them off.

Kimbers was adamant about what she wanted and what she didn't. Her wishes were really detailed: not having her hair in a toggle, no slides; how she wanted the coffin, inside and out; the horse and carriage; everyone wearing pink, even the boys; who was to carry the coffin; that her brothers sing *Dream a Little Dream*; she wanted Black Eyed Peas music but we could pick the rest; strawberries and bubbly to be served after the service.

She wanted to leave Teddy for us to look after. Teddy had been with Kimbers for ever, a special support at medical appointments and when she was in hospital. I was really touched that she wanted us to have him, but slightly sad that he wouldn't be with her. But, on reflection, I thought perhaps she wouldn't need him as much as we would.

We cried when we read her requests, but once we had finished I said that we were going to put it in a box and lock it away. I also told her that if she wanted to add anything to it or talk about it again, she just had to say.

Planning ahead doesn't mean that you're giving up; you never give up, you always have hope; you never stop chasing rainbows.

Maybe our attitude influenced Kimberley, without our being aware of it. Don't get me wrong, we didn't focus our life together on looking for alternative treatment; we tried to live normally, doing normal, everyday things. There were times when we thought about going farther afield to see what other countries, such as America, were doing; what advances were being made in the treatment of her condition. But we felt that we had to be realistic and look at the quality of not only Kimber's life but also of our other children. Did we want our lives filled up with travelling and hospital appointments, more tests and trials, and disappointment if nothing worked in the end? Not to mention the cost and having to raise money. There is no price you can put on your child's life and we would have raised the money for overseas treatments if we hadn't decided that, all things considered, to us the most important thing was to protect, as far as possible, the normal routine of our daughter's life. It was already filled with enough appointments with doctors and consultants here in England and, although there were times when we felt guilty that we were not pursuing treatments abroad, I do think we made the right decision.

Once, watching a TV programme on pulmonary hypertension,

one of the problems Kimbers had, I wrote down the name of the consultant who was speaking about the condition. I then contacted the programme and spoke to him. We had previously been told that no more could be done to ease this debilitating condition and that we must accept it. Thank goodness we didn't stop chasing those rainbows! We got referred to him and Kimberley was put on a new medication. Within a few days she was a different person, she had so much more energy. So it is important to keep looking and listening, because help can come from unusual sources.

Although she was unaware of it, Kimberly touched many people's lives and left a lasting impression on them. One of her teachers said, "She taught me so much. Never waste a moment, that was how she lived her life." Another said that, however bad a day she was having, Kimberley's strength made it possible to forget her own problems because that is what Kimbers did, she always battled on. She had such a positive outlook on life and saw the good in everything and everyone. After being in her company for only a short time Kimbers had a gift for making people feel at ease and relaxed, as if they had known her for far longer. We often used to think how familiar people were, but Kimbers accepted it as if it was the most natural thing. She seldom complained and she was always smiling; she helped put life in perspective.

Someone once said, "You can't have regrets, you knew she was going to die, and you did all the stuff you wanted to do." I suppose this was true but Kimbers had always got over all the hurdles in her path; she had defied what the professionals had predicted and had recovered from so many infections and operations that we never thought she would actually die. She had proved those clinicians wrong too many times.

When she did die it was a tremendous shock to us all. Her brother Chris told us that he hadn't thought of his sister as anything special when he was growing up, but as he got older he began to realise how amazing she was. She has been an inspiration to them both. Jamie said he never saw her as disabled, they just did normal things together, laughed and argued like other siblings. Both boys loved her so much, but they also learnt from her example and are the stronger for it.

What I have come to realise is that life is always so busy, perhaps too busy, but somehow you need to remember to take a little time out of your day to sit and read that special book with your children, praise them, have a cuddle and, if you're lucky, a kiss! Let them do your make-up or your nails, look at special photos together, share happy memories.

We're all guilty of saying, "In a minute." Looking back, it is the small, intimate things that mean so much. They don't cost anything but they are priceless. Just make time. We know life goes by too quickly, that life IS too short, so make the very most of it.

FOREVER IN OUR HEARTS
AND IN OUR MINDS.

Billy-Rose

Rachel

Francesca and
Josephine

Bethany Joy

Martin & Andrew

Andrew

Heather

Martin

Heather

Kimberley

Nicholas

Hannah

Yasmin

Gary

Cora

"It does not matter when you are born or when you die, but what you do in between is important."

Harry

Jade

Everol

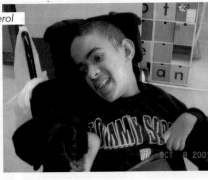

Nicholas

By his Mum

There are times in one's life when you look back and think, "Why did no one listen?"

During what seemed to be a normal pregnancy, there were several occasions when I mentioned to doctors and midwives that I felt strongly there was something wrong. In spite of assurances that all was well, these nagging doubts continued.

Our precious Nicholas was born in the early hours of Tuesday, 11th April 1995. As proud parents we could not wait to take him home. However, first he needed the routine blood and urine test. That done, we were free to go.

On the following Saturday, during a home visit from the midwife, a phone call came that changed everything. We were requested to take Nicholas to the Bristol Children's Hospital for an appointment on Monday morning with a paediatric consultant. The nagging fears returned.

That meeting confirmed those long-felt misgivings as my husband and I were informed that the tests had revealed a unique chromosomal disorder. He went on to describe a long list of symptoms and illnesses that our lovely boy would ultimately have to endure. He then added that it was unlikely Nicholas would live beyond three months.

On hearing this devastating news we were both heartbroken. The shock was so profound that I remember little of the silent journey home and it was some time before the reality of the situation sank in. When it finally did I became emotionally and mentally distraught. The fear of losing Nicholas put a barrier between us and I couldn't bond with him or think straight. My world had been turned upside down and I was no longer able to function normally. However, realising that if it looked like I could not care for him he may have to be looked after by someone else, I soon took up my role as his mother and immediately we became inseparable and there was nothing I would not do for him.

Nicholas defied the consultant's three-month prediction but as he grew older he became more and more ill and began to display the symptoms we had been told to expect. Soon, his condition had deteriorated to such a degree he was declared profoundly handicapped and terminally ill.

By this time I had come to terms with life and was, with my husband (who is also disabled), doing all of Nicholas's complex care. The cocktail of drugs he was on, the feeding regime and personal care he needed, made for a demanding, 24/7 routine. Deprived of sleep and completely exhausted I desperately needed some rest and it was at this low point that we were introduced to Little Bridge House. LBH became our oasis in the desert! The hospice had only recently opened and we were one of the first families to use it. It was a place where we could go and relax. Taking a break meant we could recharge our batteries and I could get a good night's sleep knowing that Nicholas, dearly loved by all the staff, was happy and being fully cared for.

It is almost impossible for me to describe the emotional rollercoaster I went on during the many hospital admissions and near-death incidents in Nicholas's short life. Emergencies that produced emotions from worry and anxiety, to anger at those doctors who suggested that we should let him go. I have always believed that life is a precious gift and worth fighting for and that, as Nicholas's parents, it was our duty to do just that. I also wondered if they would have suggested such a thing had it been their own son's life in the balance.

By now Nicholas was starting to defy modern medical science. Given the seriousness of his condition, doctors could not understand why he was still alive. The explanation they finally recorded in his medical notes was that he remained alive 'due to the love, care, and attention he received at home'. How very proud I felt!

Harder than caring for Nicholas was the constant fight with service and equipment providers, just to get basic service provision. This is the last thing parents caring for a seriously ill child need. The different departments and statutory agencies constantly passed us on to someone else and we often ended up seeing the person we had first contacted. It was extremely frustrating and made life very difficult.

I am aware that I have painted a very bleak picture so far, but that was only one part of our life with Nicholas. There was also the pleasure that he gave us. We took several holidays abroad to Spain, Tunisia and the Czech Republic to see my parents and relatives. They all loved our beautiful, blond, blue-eyed boy and he adored being the centre of attention. I remember strolling through a busy market with him one sunny day, the people all around came up to us, smiling and giving Nicholas sweets. He laughed and giggled all the way back. He really loved those holidays in the sun.

In 1998 a little sister came along for Nicholas. We really wanted another child and I was naturally apprehensive, but she was healthy and we were delighted with her. It can be very difficult for siblings of ill children, especially in their early years, to see all the attention being lavished on the poorly child. I always made sure that my daughter was never left out and made a conscious effort to include her in Nicholas's daily routine. Getting her to help me care for him in small ways made her feel included and they loved each other dearly.

Life can be hard when there is a severely disabled child in the family. Whether through thoughtlessness, ignorance or insensitivity people avoid you, sometimes because they don't know what to say or how to respond, and this is very hurtful. I have experienced this and our daughter was often left out of parties, social events and invitations to friends' houses, simply because of Nicholas. This seems so sad and I'm sure is due to a lack of understanding and education, but it can impact badly on siblings and their parents.

Nicholas died at Little Bridge House in 2010. We had fought hard to keep him alive and, to the last, if we could have breathed for him we would have done so. But it was not to be.

It was when he was no longer with us that we realised just how much Nicholas had taught us all over the years. He was our inspiration and we became different, I hope better, people because of him. During his lifetime I had been constantly by his side and had acquired a great deal of knowledge and nursing skills to be able to care for him on a daily basis. Looking after his complex needs had meant learning certain procedures and I did not want to lose those skills. I decided that my life would take a new direction. I had previously been employed as a Personal Assistant, but I no longer wanted an office job. Instead, I decided to become a medical support worker, looking after sick children with complex conditions, like Nicholas's.

I really love my work. I enjoy bringing comfort and happiness to the children I care for and I can thank Nicholas for all of this. Nicholas, who could not speak but told me he loved me with his eyes.

HIS LIFE WAS SHORT
BUT OH SO FULL.
THE JOY HE GAVE,
THE LOVE HE SHOWED,
WAS PLAIN FOR ALL TO SEE.

Hannah: A Conversation

By her sisters

Hannah was two years old when we were told she had Sanfilippo syndrome, in March 1995. Overnight we went from being a 'normal' family to join the world that is special needs. It took a lot of strength but we were keen for Hannah to have as 'normal' a life as possible, and when Mollie was born a year later, it was as if we had given Hannah the best present ever – I remember her coming into hospital and rushing straight past me – "baby!" she cried.

By this time, Sanfilippo had taken hold of Hannah's brain, and she was already losing skills so by the time Freya was born two years later, she took very little notice of her.

Both Mollie and Freya grew up in a world where disability was normal; both girls enjoyed this very special life and appreciated the benefits it brought them. They grew up knowing that some children die before their time and this knowledge has made them value life and become very special young women.

I'm Freya and I'm 15.

And I'm Mollie, 17.

And we're going to tell you about our sister Hannah.

She had a condition called Sanfilippo.

We'd never heard of it either. It meant that she was disabled.

But that didn't matter to us because we didn't see it as a problem.

Growing up there were some things that we couldn't do, but Mum and Dad were incredible at managing us all so we didn't miss out on much.

They must have done a good job. Just look at how we turned out!

Anyway, back to Hannah. When she was a teenager she was just the same as anybody else. She loved girlie things, was cheeky and fun to be around.

Yeah, she was her own person and knew what she liked and didn't like. Just like us.

We were the same as any other family. When she was younger we'd wait for the bus with Han, kiss her goodbye and then Mum would take us off to school.

We'd see our friends.

Visit our grandparents. Do all the normal things.

We adored Hannah and, of course, if we could have chosen for her to be born healthy then we'd have said yes.

She deserved to live a long and happy life but …

If she hadn't been who she was, we both wouldn't have experienced the fantastic life we had.

With Hannah we got to meet so many people, such as David and Christine, Julie and Chris, Libby and Liz and all the people at Little Bridge House. And we got to do lots of different things, like going to Centre Parcs, PGL and finding Santa of course, when we were much younger.

All because of her.

We had some great holidays too.

Most of our main memories with Hannah were at Disney World; that was where she looked happiest.

Every time we'd go there she'd watch the parade, look in the shops and you could see her face just light up with happiness.

We always got special treatment.

Yes, because we had Hannah we got to cut queues and go in through the back entrance.

Remember the time when David, the carer, refused to go on Thunder Mountain?

Yes, he never liked the rides, so whenever we'd want to go on one he'd put up a fuss saying, "I'll watch the wheelchair".

So we'd go on with Hannah, who'd just laugh the whole way round.

Another time we went we were taking a family photo and Hannah decided to be a cheeky monkey and try to walk off, just as we were about to take the photo.

She could be a real pickle!

In the airport we got to go onto the aeroplane first because Hannah was in a wheelchair and she had to go on a special thing to get up into it. One year this charity called Dial a Dream paid for us to stay at Give Kids the World Village in Florida over Christmas. We had a great time.

There were always Disney characters around at mealtimes, and one time Pinocchio got a bit close to Hannah and she bit his nose out of excitement. It was so funny and definitely Hannah's way of saying, "don't get too close or I'll get you". That was a great holiday, Disney World do the best chips.

Yeah, they do!

However, as Hannah got older it got to the point where we couldn't take her on holiday with us because it was too stressful, as she needed a lot of things, like certain medication and food. So she had her own holiday at Little Bridge House, but without her it felt weird because it wasn't really a family holiday.

When she first couldn't come we both felt like we couldn't properly enjoy ourselves doing the things that made her happiest.

It didn't seem right for us to be having fun without her. She loved Disney but she couldn't be with us. It was sad.

In the end we tried to be happy because that's what she would have wanted, but looking back on it now we both feel how unfair it was on her and us. Plus, we couldn't skip queues.

That too, but it was her company we missed most.

When we were at home Hannah loved watching Disney movies, especially *Aladdin* and the *Aristocats*.

We played songs from both at her funeral.

When she'd watch them she'd laugh and dance and practically looked like she was part of the movie. Another favourite film of hers was *Mary Poppins*. Whenever the chimney sweep's dance came on Mum would take hold of Hannah and dance around with her. She loved it.

Remember her favourite toy? Lady from *Lady and the Tramp*. The colour was faded and Mum had to sew the ear back on loads of times, but Han loved her so it didn't matter.

Like we said, Hannah wasn't dumb, she was independent, and if she didn't like something you'd know it.

She had her own personality, her own life, and just because she was disabled didn't mean she should be excluded from doing certain things.

She had her own way of having fun and sharing her thoughts and feelings with you.

She could be really cheeky. I remember when her key worker had her for the first time and Hannah decided to empty the entire video case in the lounge at Little Bridge and throw them at her. We all knew that she was saying, "Ha ha ha, you're in for a real treat here mate."

Another time, Hannah was being looked after by a carer who hadn't seen her since she was little, Hannah knew this and cheekily played on it. And what about the time the carer was giving her her breakfast and, as she turned to Mum to talk to her, Hannah went smack and chucked the bowl of Sugar Puffs all over the massive table and laughed her socks off.

Being a sibling of a disabled child has its ups and downs. You may think it is difficult because you don't get to experience what most children do when they're growing up. Well that is 100% wrong!

I agree, but one thing you do have to do is grow up and make your own decisions much quicker than other children may have to.

That's true. For example, the sooner we learnt to walk and feed ourselves the better because our parents had to look after Hannah. So we had to be more independent.

But on the other hand, as a family we had lots of things available to us. For example, we went to Little Bridge House for so many weeks a year. It was fantastic because we were able to spend time as a family and relax while a carer looked after Hannah.

Yes, and while we were there we weren't left out in any way because they had people who would do activities with us siblings too. We made so many friends there. My photograph is still on some of the Little Bridge leaflets – fame!

There was also a young carer's group we joined that took us on all sorts of activities. One time we went to a PGL camp with the MPS society where we got to do lots of outdoor activities with children just like us.

I suppose there were a few drawbacks.

Like what?

Well, when we were growing up we weren't able to have sleepovers because there was simply not enough room in the house because of all of Hannah's things.

And also, if something was to happen to Hannah during the night and she needed to be rushed to hospital things would then become difficult for our friend.

Yeah, but none of that really mattered.

And we didn't know any different, so we weren't bothered.

We loved having Hannah around and, although mum and dad weren't around much to play with us, we were able to play with each other and include Hannah too.

We think having Hannah around was incredible.

And it has taught us loads of things that we got to experience before any of our friends did. We got to make our own decisions.

And become more responsible.

Also now, by having the experience of Hannah, we have better skills to understand special needs children.

That helps when we volunteer at Play Scheme.

We loved Hannah so much.

We loved like any girls would love their sister and just because she was disabled didn't mean we loved her any less.

With Hannah we got to spend lots of time at Little Bridge House and without her we would never have met some of the people that matter most to us.

She was a massive part of both our lives and even now it's difficult to talk about her, but she was one of the greatest things that ever happened to us.

So, if anyone asks us if having a disabled sister was hard, we'd have to reply, "NO".

As for limitations, we just had to think of substitutions!

All the other children who have disabled brothers and sisters need to know that they shouldn't moan about the things they can't do, they should embrace the time they have together as they will not be around forever.

We miss Hannah dearly and we know that without her we wouldn't be the people we are today, and we are grateful for that.

And we'd kill to have her back!

Yasmin

If I had my time again, would I change anything.......? No, I was one of the lucky ones; I had one of the most precious things anyone could ever wish for. She may not have stayed long, but God did I love her while she was here. This may sound strange to those that have not been in this privileged position, but to know that every moment is so precious, the love you have is so intense, it can never be matched.

I can rest now, knowing that we gave all we possibly could to Yasmin, we made her life as happy as it could be. She was surrounded by people who loved her. Life was fun and she made the most of every opportunity to leave her mark. It is hard to think of her without smiling.

How do I begin to describe my gorgeous Yasmin? She was cheeky, naughty, wicked, funny. She loved slapstick humour. If anyone fell over, hurt themselves, or cried, she thought it was hilarious. She loved the words, "No, Yasmin". She loved to leave a wake of destruction in her path.

No one was allowed any accessories because they would be pinched, tweaked, poked, twanged or removed.

No one ever forgot her, from the professors at Great Ormond Street, whose pens, aprons, masks, glasses and name badges were all removed within seconds, to poor unsuspecting people walking around the shops, who were groped while they bent over to look at something.

She would not settle unless she had her Barney videos playing, some nibbles in her bowl and a 'clippy' in her hand to open and close. She never moaned or complained and hardly ever cried. She put up with pain, being scared, feeling ill, being away from home and the rest of the family, and she rose above it all with dignity. She made the best of every situation. In fact, many of us could learn a valuable lesson from children like Yasmin.

We all remember her with a smile, because she had a ball while she was here. She followed no rules, she lived for the moment and the stimulation of being alive. She would walk into freezing cold sea, squirt herself full pelt in the face with a hose, giggle to herself, then do it again!

She loved animals because they understood her, they were always so calm and gentle with her and would put up with her manhandling without complaint. Except for the poor pigeon that, after landing on her pushchair expecting some bread, got picked up by the head. He did survive, just slightly ruffled.

Other children adored her because she was fun. She would do all the outrageous things that they would love to, like throwing a dozen eggs on the floor, one at a time, out of the fridge door! Doing rude raspberries in the middle of a christening when the vicar had waffled on just a bit too long. Spitting, laughing, shouting whenever or wherever she liked, even all night long if the moon was full.

But that was our Yaz, you couldn't be cross. Don't get me wrong, I was tearing my hair out most of the time, but life is for living and she certainly did.

Making memories to keep

If I had my time again I would make sure to make more keepsakes.

I never took enough photos of my three children together. It was before digital cameras, so the ones I have haven't captured them as I wished they had.

I have videos, but not enough. They are so precious, even if you never watch them, it's just reassuring to know they are there if ever you need them and, believe me, one day you will.

Footprints and handprints, hair, teeth, teddies, clothes, anything physical that you can hold, touch, smell or cuddle.

Sometimes it is hard to believe that she ever existed and I just have to go up into the loft and hold her clothes, smell them and close my eyes, remember the physical Yasmin. I feel inside her boots where her little feet had made footprints, or rub her silky lock of hair on my cheek. She was here. She really was here with me.

Make special places, somewhere you all love, somewhere you have fun together, somewhere you always remember with a smile. Yasmin loved animals, so we went to the zoo for her birthday every year, and still do. It's a lovely thing to do and I'm sure she still comes with us because the animals always seem to look behind me.

Songs are so important, they never go away and you can listen to them whenever you need a moment to remember. Be ready though, because they will always catch you out at the wrong moment. When Yasmin first went I never listened to the radio because I never knew what would play, so I stuck to CDs. You just had to be on your guard when out in shops, restaurants, hairdressers, anywhere where one of your special songs might play. Now I see it as a coincidence and listen to the lyrics to see what message she is trying to send me. But it is nine years since we had our last dance, so I have become much braver.

Living One Day At A Time

In a way, I feel so lucky to have known how precious every moment with Yasmin was. It changes your whole way of thinking, your whole outlook on life. I didn't plan for the future, I never put anything off until another day. Today could have been the last day we were together and I didn't want to be left with any regrets about the things I should have done differently. I would hear on the news about people losing loved ones, suddenly, with no warning. I would feel blessed to have been given the chance to make the best job of our lives.

My priorities changed. I got on and remarried and, luckily, I met someone who understood and was happy for me to give every last ounce of my love and energy to Yasmin. I knew that with his support I could have more children and give Yasmin a proper family. Give her an escape from all the treatments and procedures and hospitalisation she had to endure.

It was the best thing I ever did. She adored her little sister Indi and brother Robin; they had a deep connection and understanding that no one else could be part of. The little ones accepted her without question, that's all they had known and, in their little lives, it was the norm. Children have a lovely ability to see past disabilities and medical equipment. They grew up learning to dodge the pinches and donks on the head, all given in love but quite painful at times.

The games they played and the fun they had together were magical to watch and couldn't be captured on film, but are in my memory and the children's hearts forever.

I never kept any information from Indi or Robin, I was always honest with them and told them what I thought they needed to know. I knew how important it was for me to know Yasmin could leave us at any time. I wanted them to have the same opportunity to do and say all they needed to, before she went.

I remember Indi going through a phase, when she was five and Yasmin was ten, of sleeping on a mattress next to Yasmin's bed. They would fall asleep holding hands, then wake up giggling together.

We didn't live in doom and gloom, quite the opposite, we had a great time. We let Yasmin experience as much as she could. She wasn't treated any differently to the others, as much as was possible, with her special needs and illness. Most of the time she was just one of the gang, subject to all the discipline and house rules that any family has. In the back of my mind I always had a little voice telling me she was no more precious than the others, because any of them could go at any time, she was just the one we knew about.

Friends you lose and friends you gain

I have always believed that people come into our lives at certain times for a particular purpose, whether it is to educate us, support us, love us or guide us. But they also leave our lives when they have served their purpose. Not necessarily consciously, it is just how it is. Even with this belief it has been very hard to go through, even heartbreaking at times.

Friends I thought I had for life, ones I had known all my growing up years, ones I had helped through their own traumas, baled out on me. They couldn't cope with the thought of Yasmin being terminally ill. Some would make excuses, others wouldn't call any more and others would just disappear without explanation.

At the other end of the scale, my life was enriched with loving, caring people with empathy, who genuinely cared about my family and me.

Our life put everyone under immense strain for years and years; times could be so desperate but then be full of jubilation. It was a rollercoaster and some amazing people were there for the whole ride.

It was always hard letting others into your family life, they would see your raw emotions, they would be there for the most desperate, traumatic times in your life. I used to get upset for Yasmin when different medical staff, school staff or carers would become so close to her, she would form a close bond with them, learn to love and trust them, then they would leave and I could see her pain, and we would have to start all over again.

It is very hard to keep everything in perspective when you are in the middle of that rollercoaster ride. I can see now that people looking in from the outside have to stay detached to a certain degree, for their own self-preservation. They need to be able to deal with the next little one like Yasmin.

A positive from every negative

When I lost Yasmin, I was determined that she wouldn't die in vain. She had always been so strong and such an inspiration so, with her help, I am going to use what I learnt and make a difference.

From every negative situation you can always get a positive effect. However hard and desperate it seems at the time, it is teaching us life's lessons, ones that will stay with us and change our way of thinking forever, and give us the ability to empathise with other people in similar situations.

I remember thinking that my situation couldn't get any worse and there was no way I would get through it. Often, as fate would have it, it would get worse and, with the help of all the amazing people around me, I would get through it. Coming out the other end stronger and more resilient.

It is amazing what you can survive and still smile and continue to live your life. But, instead of wasting it moaning about trivial rubbish and wallowing in self-pity, live it to the full, embrace every moment. You know you can survive anything life throws at you; it's a good feeling, to be indestructible.

Fate has put you here to deal with this, so do it in style and come out the other end a better person, with something to offer other people. You really can make a difference to someone's life; you could be the one person that gets them through it.

THE MORE DIFFICULT THE JOURNEY,
THE MORE CHERISHED THE MEMORIES.

Gary
By Tracie

If you ask any expectant mother what she wants her baby to be, she will invariably answer, "I don't mind whether it's a girl or a boy, as long as it's healthy." I was no different and when Gary was born in 1988 his father and I were thrilled with our son. He was handsome and healthy, or so we thought.

As he grew there were some health concerns but it was not until he was four that he was diagnosed with Duchenne muscular dystrophy. It was at this point that our lives were torn apart.

What made it even worse was the reaction of our families. They didn't seem to understand that what had happened to Gary could happen to anyone. It was what the specialist called, "a rogue gene". They all got into the blame game. My family thought it must be Stuart's 'fault' and when it was proved that it was more likely to have come from my side, they just didn't want to know. It seemed that, whatever the outcome, no one was going to be happy. Friends too drifted away when they realised Gary had a condition that was not going to be fixed. So that left Stuart and I coping on our own. This was to become the pattern of our life together and, I suppose, the reason why we have became such fighters.

Looking back though, it's sad to think that the people who had been so delighted at the birth of our son were now turning their backs on us. We hadn't changed and our lovely boy was still the same, but because he wouldn't grow up to do all the things other children did he was being shunned. As if it was his fault. Perhaps the terrible news was too much for them. I certainly don't think any of them can have really thought it through. I hope people are now a bit more aware, and sympathetic, and realise the terrible hurt their actions caused, but I doubt it somehow. Anyway, we just had to get on with our lives and we were frankly far too busy to dwell on it then. But the hurt went deep.

Over the following years we learnt much about this destructive disease and were devastated to learn that it was a terminal illness. However, once we had absorbed the shock, we decided to focus on making Gary's life as fulfilled and happy as possible. He was a naturally contented boy who took most things in his stride, popular with his peers and adults alike. He was not one to make a fuss or require any kind of special treatment; he just wanted to get on with his life.

It was a life of hospital appointments and admissions but he seemed to cope with it all. We found the constant changes in the system frustrating, although I understood the difficulties. There was little continuity of care and it was hard to find a doctor or specialist who really listened and understood your situation and then find you were having to see someone new and repeat everything you had said so many, many times before.

Getting a house adapted to Gary's increasing needs was another nightmare. We were offered a house and the ground floor was adapted to include a bedroom and bathroom, just what we needed. Then we discovered that they had included a small entrance hall, too narrow for the wheelchair to go through. Nothing is ever perfect I know, and we did laugh about it later, but it took us three years to get it changed!

Meanwhile, Stuart was earning himself a reputation. I was advised by a professional to go to meetings on my own as he was sometimes, "too demanding". This was because he was fighting to maintain his son's independence for as long as possible by demanding the equipment that was needed in order to achieve it. What father wouldn't fight for his son? I was proud of him and we continued to go to meetings together.

Meantime, we were blessed with Andrew, Jamie and Natasha, siblings for Gary; a complete family. When Gary was ten we were thrown a lifeline in the form of a referral to the children's hospice, where we were able to recharge our batteries, spend time with the children and relax. Gary loved the place, taking full advantage of all the amenities it offered, the computer games, the remote controlled cars, he enjoyed all the wonderful things in the house. But the best thing about it was making new friends.

Francis, a member of the care team, who came to know us well over the years, wrote fondly of Gary:

> *One of my most endearing memories of him involves the Bingo sessions. These were held in the dining room after supper and were legendary! Families would gather around the huge table, the youngsters eagerly eyeing up the mound of prizes displayed at one end. It was here that Gary's selfless side showed through. When he won he would seldom choose something for himself, rather letting his younger siblings choose what they wanted. In fact if there were any young ones without a prize he'd give them his. There was never any fuss made, he just did it in the way he did everything, quietly smiling.*

Yes, he was a very special boy and I'm not saying this just because one Easter, when he had won the huge chocolate egg, he insisted on giving it to me. Honest!

When Gary was ill, and these incidents became more and more frequent, he would still try to get on with normal life and never played on his illness. He particularly loved the Teenage weekends and, just before he died, he was at Little Bridge House with his friends, enjoying the treats and outings on offer. Although his health at this time was putting him more at risk he was determined to go. He was particularly looking forward to the trip that had been arranged to a football match in Yeovil. It was a bitterly cold November day and he had been very unwell the day before. Staff did their best to dissuade him from going, trying to tempt him with the thought of having the whole house to himself, being given a Jacuzzi (which he loved) and all manner of treats, but all to no avail. Gary had made up his mind, he was going.

The trip meant a travelling time of four and a half hours, which no doubt proved agony for the accompanying carers. I knew they would have been well prepared for any emergency with oxygen, a suction machine, sick bowls and numerous blankets to keep them all, not just Gary, as warm as possible. I learnt later that during the journey the carers never took their eyes off him to make sure there were no signs of change or discomfort. It was the same during the match, they didn't watch the football but, alarmed at how pale he had become, couldn't wait to get back to the bus. They made it back to the house, to everyone's great relief, and Gary declared he was so pleased he went because it had been "brilliant!"

We were pleased too because, just two weeks later, he died.

We were devastated and, despite eight years having passed, miss him just as much as on that first terrible day. He was a very special boy whose quiet courage and determination impressed all those who knew him. He never complained about his life and accepted that there were things he would never do, but this did not stop him enjoying life. He will always be remembered as a remarkable young man.

What of our lives now? Well, Gary turned us into fighters and we have continued to fight since his brother, Jamie, has special needs. I'm happy to record that after a considerable struggle we have won him a place in just the right school for the best education he could get, so we can relax – for the moment.

NO MATTER WHAT
LIFE THREW AT HIM
HE JUST GOT ON WITH IT,
ALWAYS WITH A SMILE.

Cora
By Marian

I don't think any of my adult life has turned out quite the way I had expected it to. Born in the 50s and growing up through the 60s there was a lot of change in all things, science, society, politics. The older generation found it shocking with the memory of the recent world wars so vivid. But for me, this was my world, it was okay, it was normal.

I had never anticipated living in London, it did not beckon or entice me. Further education and work led me to many towns and rural communities across the UK. But then, I met the man who was to become my husband and moved to London, where we lived in sin. This caused embarrassment for my parents, but not for me. It took several years for my other half to pop the question. The next steps were very logical and obvious to me. You buy a house and have babies. Well, neither of those things happened quite as I'd thought they would.

We discovered we could only afford to buy a studio flat in London so we moved to Bristol. The same week we bought our first house a friend of my husband's family died and left us a house in west London. See what I mean about unexpected?

Both houses, over 100 miles apart, were projects. A challenge. Still, we rolled up our sleeves and learnt the joy of DIY! The babies didn't happen. We waited, we relaxed, we got on with life, we did DIY, but no babies.

The Bristol house was finished before the London one, so we sold it and moved to London. I was referred to a London fertility clinic. It wasn't easy. Drugs, procedures, investigations, timing.

It grinds you down. Just when it looked like we were at the end of the baby road, with only very expensive IVF holding out any hope, I got pregnant. Yes, I had had my vale of tears, the difficult bit was behind me. We were on the up.

My husband and I were very excited. I loved being pregnant. I did all the bits the baby books said. It was normal. Everyone was pleased for us. We bought things for a nursery and argued over names. Then, in March, two weeks after the due date, my labour started and we went off to the maternity unit.

Yep, you've guessed, it was not the normal birth I had been expecting. My daughter was an undiagnosed breech birth and I had an emergency caesarean in the middle of the night. All those NTC lessons were to no avail.

I ended up in a ward of six newly-delivered mums early the next morning. We did all the things we were asked. Our babies cried and fed and cried and slept, but mine did not poo. Doctors came and looked anxious and asked questions. Yes, she had been sick. But didn't all babies regurgitate food? More doctors, worried faces. And she was taken to the special care baby unit. They took a Polaroid photo of her and asked me her name. They gave me the picture and told me to say goodbye. WHAT WAS GOING ON!

The doctors thought my daughter had a bowel blockage and needed to go to Great Ormond Street Hospital to get sorted out. My husband could travel in the ambulance with her but, having had a caesarean, I would have to stay behind at the maternity hospital.

It was late at night when my husband came back and said that cystic fibrosis had been talked about. I sat in a room full of women nursing their babies and asked did anyone know about cystic fibrosis. Someone volunteered they had flag days and charity box collections, but that was it.

I walked around the hospital for most of that night. I was in a bad place. Tired by the morning, I rested on my bed. A midwife came to me and asked me crossly where my baby was. When I told her Great Ormond Street Hospital (GOS), things started to happen. I was whisked out of the ward into a room of my own, with an empty cot in the corner. I was told I would have to wait to join my daughter. The doctors had to be sure I was okay before sending me out into the world. It took three very long days, during which time our baby had a bowel operation to remove a blockage, re-lay her bowel and remove her appendix.

When I saw her, I cried. I loved her so much. I missed her. Tubes and wires plugged into her little body were attached to machines that flashed and bleeped. I was not allowed to hold her and could only touch her once every three hours. My husband and I had to take turns. I sat in a chair and just looked at her.

As she became stronger I was allowed to hold her more often, but it felt that this was not my child. She belonged to the hospital, to the nurses and the doctors, not to us as parents.

Instead of me, the nurses changed her nappies, and clothes, and bathed her face in special water that came in clear little sachets, and when I kissed her she tasted salty. I wondered what was in the water from those sachets.

We were told that 95% of babies with the problems our daughter had were suffering with cystic fibrosis, but we wouldn't know for sure until the test results came through. Well, I thought that was a 5% chance of being okay. Everything else that had happened to us was unusual, short odds. You never know.

No, you never do. The results came back and cystic fibrosis was confirmed.

Slowly my daughter got stronger and she was moved from intensive care to a room on another ward. I had been living in the hospital with her and in this room we felt a little more okay, a unit. I held her close a lot. She liked my company, I liked hers.

I asked about cystic fibrosis, or CF, a great deal. The news came back jumbled and contradictory but none of it was good, not good at all. We were told we could not take her home until we had seen the CF doctors, who were away at a conference. We were given booklets that didn't seem to relate to our beautiful baby girl.

After that truly horrible start to our new phase in life, things settled down a bit. Having a baby makes life so different. There is so much to learn, so much theory to put into practice. The regime for daily CF care just became part of that learning curve. As with the houses, we just rolled up our sleeves and got on with it. Twice-daily chest physio and enzymes with all food became normal, for us. My father had had a lifelong illness, rheumatoid arthritis, so I'd already experienced how life just went on, but with some allowances to accommodate his illness. Everybody worked, everybody played, life went on and this was ours. So CF was part of our lives and we just got on with it.

CF is a genetically inherited disease. You need two carrier parents to make a child with CF. We needed to tell our families about this, they could have this problem too. The news had a very mixed reception, from, "Oh well, we'll just see what we are sent," to, "It's all your fault."

My daughter grew and did all the things she should do. She attended playgroup, went on holiday, had fun. She started nursery, went to school. Always, I explained about CF and her needing enzymes before food. Some people got it and some didn't. I knew that some had labelled me as a fussy mother.

In reception the teacher asked if she was getting enough sleep? She was falling asleep in class and hardly ate anything. I knew that and was really worried. By the time she was five and a half she was very poorly and ended up back in GOS while they tried to find out what the trouble was. Three weeks of tests showed nothing and it became clear that the medics thought I was the problem. But then, by a stroke of luck, they discovered that she actually had a very unusual medical problem and was so ill she could die. After more, very aggressive, surgery she made it home in time for Christmas. Her problems were caused by a new drug, they thought. She became much better and began to grow. We had a few more normal years, honest.

One thing that had always been part of the deal for me was more children, both for my sake and my child's. For every pregnancy, for a couple who carry the CF gene, there is a 25% chance of CF and therefore a 75% chance of no CF. I liked those odds a lot. I had become pregnant once and could do it again, and if we got a baby with CF, well, we knew what we were doing this time so it wouldn't be that much of a problem.

What's that saying? Man makes plans and God laughs? I think I am probably his personal stand-up comedian.

Nothing worked and we ended up on a new trial for families affected by genetically inherited diseases. Embryos created through IVF were tested for the inherited disease before being implanted. It didn't work. Our daughter was now six and quite clear. She wanted a brother or sister and would we please get one. We felt the only way left was to adopt. We spoke to her about it and she understood and was enthusiastic.

Here we were, on another unexpected journey. We were given some help from the parents of our daughter's best friend from school. They had adopted her from Romania. We were keen for a UK adoption and had been told it would be difficult and, boy oh boy, was it! By now we were both in our forties and during the assessment process it became clear to us we were, you name it we were too it: too old, too young, too dark skinned, too fair skinned, not blond, too middle class, not mixed race, not ethnic, not English (my husband's parents were Polish refugees from the Second World War, my father was Irish). It went on and on.

Eventually we were accepted as being a suitable family, but there were no suitable children, I think because we were 'too' everything. Unless, of course, we would like disruptive boys with behavioural problems, or an older, brain-damaged child. We would definitely not be eligible for a child any younger than five and it would be a child with special needs. How would it be for the adopted child to have an older sibling with CF? Our social worker got pregnant and we got a new one, who clearly didn't like us. It went on and on and on.

After four years I was wondering just how much more I could cope with. We had been thoroughly examined, had had every aspect of our lives and personalities gone over with a fine-toothed comb. Maybe I should call a halt to it all and just get a dog. The problem was, our daughter wanted a brother or a sister AND a dog.

I gave myself until Christmas and then a decision had to be made.

Out of blue we got a telephone call from our adoption agency, which was becoming increasingly rare. They had details of an 18-month-old boy with CF, would we like to see the forms? WOULD WE? You bet!

The forms were all about CF as a disease, not about the child. We asked many, many questions. He was not going to be advertised in the various adoption newspapers and magazines, as he was so good-looking they would be inundated with enquires. They sent a photograph. Wow, he was a looker. A gorgeous little blond boy.

Two social workers visited us from over 250 miles away, on a very snowy day, to see if we would do. They brought a video of this lovely little boy playing about in his foster home. My daughter looked so happy and said, "That's my little brother." My husband cried. And me? I panicked, which I was told was completely normal. Two months later we travelled north to meet and pick up our new son.

I can honestly say that we have absolutely no regrets about our decision. The children fight and argue and love each other in equal measure. There are nine years between them and my daughter definitely knows how to bring up boys, and it's not the way I do it.

Family life goes on, filled with holidays and hobbies, celebrations and events, school and homework, and lots and lots of hospital appointments. They both attend the same hospital and there are many new advances in treatment for CF.

We go to Australia for a family wedding and my daughter is a bridesmaid. It is such a lovely time. She turns 17 and becomes too old for the children's hospital so we now travel to the adult hospital of her choosing, an hour and a half's drive away.

Family life goes on. Hard work but we love it. We love our children, we do all the treatment required, we plough on. We are normal, but we are different. We are used to this and so are some of our friends.

After her twentieth birthday my daughter's health begins to go downhill. We are told about lung transplants and how difficult it is to get on the list. The next few months are busy and scary, many tests, many meetings, many decisions. A wheelchair is becoming part of our normal life. Two months before she is 21 she is accepted on to the transplant list. We pack her bag and wait for the call. She gets worse, and worse, and worse. She is admitted to hospital; I am allowed to stay with her; I stay for eight weeks. My husband and son bring our caravan close to the hospital to be with her. My daughter dies.

I cannot begin to explain just how difficult this is on so many fronts. It is not something you get over, or move on from, but you learn to live with the fact that it has happened. Once love has grown it never goes. With the passage of time I appreciate much, much more who she was and what she did. She achieved a lot, her life affected so many people and her positive attitude brought about many good things, she continues to give to us. It is only two and half years since she died and I am still so sad. I miss her a lot and think of her daily. We are still in contact with her boyfriend and his family. We have new and understanding friends.

My son is also not well but is lucky enough to have the right genetic make-up to take advantage of some of the new treatments on offer. This is good. We look to the future with no firm plans and try to take each day as it comes.

But what would I rather have had? A childless, CF-free life, or a life full of love and adventure and the unexpected? I know my answer, like I know the love I have for both my children will never die.

A teacher once commented that our family had a positive can-do attitude. Being unwell is not so unusual, but it's how you live with it that defines your life. My daughter did GCSEs, A levels, a BTEC and was going to start a degree in drama. We travelled to Ireland, France, Spain and Australia on holiday. She went skiing and on an outward bound trip. She enjoyed swimming and horse riding. She had a boyfriend, she learnt to drive and thought nothing of negotiating the North Circular in the rush hour. She lived a full life, but one very different from others. It is the people who understand it is normal to be different that make sense out of life. It does not matter when you are born or when you die, but what you do in between that is important.

I HAVE LEARNT THAT ONE DAY AT
A TIME IS GOOD AND YOU REALLY DO ONLY
HAVE THIS MOMENT TO LIVE IN. SO SEIZE
THE DAY AND LIVE YOUR LIFE.

Tales with Harry

By Susie

The eventful trip to See Paul Rankin

It was the summer holidays and the days ahead stretched out like beads on a string. Much prayer would certainly be needed to survive that was for sure, but I knew that it would be a colourful set of beads and there would be joy in and among their length.

The department store, John Lewis, was coming to the new shopping mall and I was excited at the thought of seeing a food demonstration by Paul Rankin. I told Jack and Sophie that seeing Paul was going to be my treat for the summer. As I expected, I was met with groans at the thought of a cooking demonstration. But, selfish or not, I wanted to go. So we all got ready and arrived in plenty of time, and even got front row seats. I parked Harry's wheelchair in the aisle next to my chair and sat down with great anticipation. After a while I thought I would take Harry out of his chair and give him a stretch on my lap. Ha! As I lifted Harry up from his chair I caught a whiff, my heart sank. Out from the bottom of his trousers ran a trail of diarrhoea, all over me and all over the floor. A giggling Harry roared with laughter. If I didn't know better I could have sworn he had timed this one.

We left with heads bowed in disgrace after hastily trying to wipe the brand new John Lewis floor with baby wet wipes. Harry giggled all the way home and Jack and Sophie praised him for his perfect timing. They were delighted to be going home to do far more enjoyable things. I returned to a pile of washing, but at least I had caught a glimpse of Paul Rankin!

Pregnancy

We were thrilled when we found out we were expecting our second child and couldn't wait to relive the wonder of our firstborn's first scan, seeing the heart and limbs beating and moving. Awesome! We arrived at the hospital in great excitement. Little did we know that what we were about to experience would alter our lives forever.

As the sonographer spent longer and longer alarm bells started ringing: what was going on? Even though we anticipated bad news, we were still shocked when she said that she had found something and we needed to see the doctor to talk through our options. It was very clear that in her mind there was no option but a clear-cut solution of an abortion. This was not a road Steve and I wanted to go down. From there on in, month by month, the news seemed to get worse and worse; a cyst on the brain then turned to water on the brain, then concerns over the size of his head compared to the rest of his growth. It became increasingly hard to see our child as a person rather than a set of problems, so we asked to find out the sex of our child. Somehow, we felt that maybe this would help us bond better if we knew and named our child. We were having a boy. Naming a child is a big responsibility. We liked the name Harry and when it turned out to mean 'fighter' we felt it was right for our son. The regular scans continued with their toll of bad news, until at week 23 we were told to anticipate a spontaneous miscarriage because the water levels surrounding Harry had reduced so much they felt it would be very likely he would die in the next week. We went home distraught, not least because we were about to lose our child but that, having travelled this far into the pregnancy, his life would not even be recognised or registered as a stillbirth. Legally, because abortion is possible up until week 24, no baby that has died in utero can be registered as stillborn until after week 24. Instead, it is added to the mother's notes as a miscarriage. But Harry, our little fighter, carried on surviving in a very small sac of fluid, growing in minuscule amounts, and was delivered by C-Section at 38 weeks, weighing in at 3lbs 2ozs. As I came round from the anaesthetic the first words that Steve said about Harry were, "He's just like Jack was. They're like peas in a pod!"

Harry's favourite things

- Bumpy paths
- Rustling paper
- A jiggling knee
- Rubbing his chest
- Chime bells
- Poo!
- Dancing Elmo
- The colour red
- Bath time
- But most of all, people.

Harry's pet hates

There were only three things, that we found, that Harry consistently hated. He made us laugh, or cringe with embarrassment, because his response was always so honest.

1. *The church organ*: very rarely was the church organ played at church. We mainly had a music group with guitars, keyboard and drums, but on the odd occasion when the organ was played

Harry consistently cried; he was obviously not impressed and made his dislike clearly known. At school one day they were using different sounds to engage Harry in movement and some he responded to with real animation, but we all cracked up when they played organ music and he went completely rigid and would not move a muscle. I am convinced he didn't want to even cry because he knew that that would activate the sound beam and make it appear that he liked the noise. That's our boy!

2. *A sermon that went on too long:* Harry had an inbuilt timer for how long he thought a sermon should be and if he thought it was going on a bit he made it very clear. A loud yawning would start to come from him, and not just one as a little hint but continuously. Funnily enough, the preacher was often unaware but our friends up in the music group would look down and smile, then the smiles would become smothered giggles and we would have to take Harry out before we disgraced everyone.

3. *The optician:* it was a complete shock to us when Harry, who was a people lover, took a distinct dislike to the hospital optician, before she did anything to him. Even I could see his reaction to her was not good. He was not listening and being still, which was his usual response with new people; he was turning his head away as if trying to be as far away as possible. When she actually came close and started to test his eyes, he did the exact opposite of what he needed to do. At no point would he comply with her wishes. The first time I didn't take too much notice, but when it happened at each subsequent visit it became too obvious to ignore. Then on another visit Harry had a different optician, he became a model patient!

Angels?

As Harry grew too heavy to carry upstairs we needed to think through safety plans for him sleeping downstairs. One of those safety plans was a camera monitor so we both hear and see him. I remember on many an occasion being woken to the sounds of those regular night visitors: pain-filled tears, seizures or sickness. But I also remember the beautiful awakenings to laughter. Harry never seemed to wake grumpy. There was one occasion I will always remember. I don't know what woke me but I remember looking at the monitor and seeing Harry's face with a look of pure enchantment all over it. He was looking up and around the ceiling, peacefully smiling, followed by smiles that turned to giggles. I couldn't help but wonder, was Harry seeing angels? Fanciful? Maybe, but one of the things that was so special about Harry was the wholeness of his spirit. His body may have been 'broken' but his spirit wasn't. It was strong, peaceful, resilient, and very sensitive to the things of God, and I feel sure that Harry knew what it was to be loved by God and to return that love.

Another near-death experience

We had many near-death experiences throughout Harry's life, but one in particular stands out.

Harry was fed via a tube and getting his hydration levels right was a difficult task; too much and he would be sick, too little and he would be constipated. Add any slight illness into the mix and it could end in a visit to the hospital because of dehydration, which in itself could cause Harry to be sick. On this particular occasion Harry just wasn't picking up and we started to notice that he was looking a little orange. The doctors did tests which showed that he had a problem with his liver, quite a serious one.

They gave him all the help they could, but finally we were told that Harry had complete liver failure and it was only a matter of days. The hospital was amazing and kitted us out in a special family room, just off the main ward.

I don't remember a great deal about that time but I do remember a hospital photographer coming to take some 'last photos' of us with Harry. We all look ghastly. Family and friends came to say their last goodbyes. We eventually decided that we would journey to Little Bridge House so we could all be together more easily and in an atmosphere that was more suited to everyone's needs. We really prayed that Harry would survive the journey. We said some tearful goodbyes, especially to the nurses who had been so wonderful in caring for Harry, and set off. After breaking the speed limit many times over, we all breathed a sigh of relief when we finally arrived. A week later, including yet more 'last photos', Harry woke up and started mouthing for food. He hadn't eaten by mouth for ten years, but it was obvious he was hungry and that he wanted to live, not die! So, little by little, we started giving Harry fluids and, little by little, he started to recover. His liver started to heal itself and Harry fought his way back to life. It took the rest of us a bit longer to recover emotionally and get back on track, but we did, and proceeded to have three more years with Harry. The consultant said it was truly miraculous. What a gift!

Jack and Sophie

Life as Harry's siblings was not plain sailing. He may not have broken up their dens or stolen their chocolate, but his presence was well and truly felt. Many a trip would be cancelled because of a seizure or sickness. Parent time that should have been shared was not shared fairly, however hard we tried. And yet Jack and Sophie showed extraordinary acts of kindness, pride and love towards Harry. When he was young Jack loved showing off Harry's ability to giggle uncontrollably if you rubbed his chest. It was as if Jack, even from a very young age, desperately wanted people to see the person behind the disabled body. Today, Jack would say that there is simply much too much to distil about all that Harry has given him and taught him.

Sophie loved to nurse and care for Harry and earned the title of the Medicine Queen for often helping me administer Harry's medicines down his stomach tube. I remember being woken by Harry's laughter on many occasions, but one in particular was when Sophie had climbed into bed with him. It was lovely to listen and watch her chat and talk with her brother, just doing what siblings do, hang out together.

What stands out very strongly for me with Jack and Sophie and their relationship with Harry was that they never seemed to be ashamed or embarrassed by him. They never wanted to distance themselves from him when friends came round or when people visited. If anything, it was just the opposite. They wanted to draw people in close to Harry, and to include Harry in all that we did. When I said this to Sophie her reaction said it all, she just looked very puzzled at me and said, "Well no! Why would we? He was our brother."

After death

When Harry died I didn't miss him so much as I missed me. It felt that with Harry's death the person I was died too. That is not to say that I didn't mourn Harry, of course I did, but the intensity and agony of that came later.

Three images helped me in my grief: the lady of Vladimir icon; the imagery of a caterpillar changing into a butterfly; and the biblical story of Jesus taking the little children in his arms and blessing them.

I identified profoundly with the cocoon stage, where everything inside goes to smoosh. That was me, the outside was intact but inside all was smoosh, a jumble. What was my identity? What was my purpose and reason in life? During this phase I felt acutely the need to guard and protect myself. I couldn't afford to let my fragile cocoon be broken or exposed because I needed to re-form within it.

I would sit for quite long periods of time in those early days. Energy levels were low and my arms would physically ache with the pain of no longer having Harry to hold. As I sat I would imagine myself safely sitting on the lap of Christ; I felt just like a small child. I would gaze at the icon of Mary holding baby Jesus and remember holding Harry. The tears would start to fall and I let them. God's power is made perfect in weakness, the Bible says. I had to enter into the weakness, embrace the weakness and become like a little child. In that weak place it was as if Christ and Harry taught me how to be weak. I remember whispering to God, "I can't do this on my own." His words of love whispered back, "I never asked you to, or ever wanted you to. I've only ever wanted to walk this life with you."

I think Harry knew about including God. For example, in times of acute pain he would cry out and then withdraw into himself. While you could tell he still had pain he would somehow be able to bear it. Maybe he, too, was imagining sitting on Christ's lap.

Before Harry's death, as I washed and held his 'broken' body I was daily reminded of the parts in me which were 'broken' too. My disabilities, I learnt, are just as real but hidden on the inside, whereas Harry's were exposed for all to see. I learnt a lot from my teacher Harry, but the greatest thing he taught me was how to keep my gaze on God; Harry's face always seemed turned to Christ. Many people have asked me how I have kept my faith. I simply don't know how to live without God. Besides, turning away from God would also mean turning away from all that Harry has taught me; both God and Harry are way too precious for that. I am now in the process of training to be a priest. Harry's life and death have had a huge part to play in bringing me to this place and I am forever grateful.

"HERE COMES DADDY WITH
A POCKETFUL OF PLUMS
...ALL FOR HARRY."

A ditty recited nightly by
Steve with Harry sitting on his
lap, gurgling with delight.
A cherished memory.

Jade
By Debbie

When I was asked to write about Jade, my first thought was to rush out and buy a pad and pen. You see, I'm a good speaker but I don't do writing. I always left that to Jade. She was the one who could put thoughts and feelings into just the right words, not me. I never know where to begin.

Jade died five years ago but her room is just the same as when she left it. I often go there to feel close to her and so it was in there that I decided not to buy anything new but to use her favourite pen and her writing pad. Who knows, she may inspire me. Although it feels strange, holding her pen in my hand, it feels nice and so, here goes.

Jade was born on the 13th October 1990, three weeks early and weighing just over four pounds. While she was in the special care unit they found she had a low platelet count, but it was not until she was sixteen weeks old that they discovered she had a heart condition. The paediatric consultant suggested a heart specialist from Southampton should come and see her. They suspected a hole in the heart so she was taken to Southampton hospital for tests. These revealed they were right and that she also had a condition called hypoplastic left heart syndrome. That was rare and far worse.

I clearly remember the meeting when we received the diagnosis. I sat there listening to them saying, "Jade is unlikely to live beyond her late teens," and thinking that this could not be happening to me, to us! I tried to block out the words but they kept coming, "Her only chance might be a heart and lung transplant."

What a diagnosis! How were we going to cope? Somehow we did and we all made the very most of what each day offered, and got on with life.

Over the years Jade spent a lot of time in hospital, but she never did have the transplant operation. She didn't want to have someone else's heart anyway. She always felt that the love she had for everyone came from her heart and since it was an essential part of who she was, she really wanted to keep it! As it turned out she wouldn't have been strong enough to undergo the operation.

As Jade grew, her character formed. She was always calm. Even in an emergency when I was rushing round gathering her things, she would be quietly chatting to the paramedics. When lying ill in hospital her thoughts were always on the other children in the ward, or checking that everyone at home, particularly her grandparents, were okay. This was how she was from a young age and as she grew older it was usual for people to remark on how wise and unselfish she was. It was the most natural thing in the world for her to put others first.

She was always positive and loved life. She celebrated the special times, like Christmas, with real delight. She lived very much in the present and was content with what life gave her. She never got disappointed or complained about what she could not do; rather, she enjoyed what she could do. Simple things pleased her, like bringing me and her dad breakfast in bed – a regular treat until she became too ill; teaching her brother Jack to bake; bird watching; walks in her Nan's flower garden; being taught to knit; doing puzzles; or, best of all, having a cup of tea and a chat about the olden days with her Grandad Crumble. These were the things she enjoyed in her easy-going way.

We both loved animals and shared our home with the rabbit, the fish and Tig, her dog that she adored, and my two dogs. They were her great joy and, however ill she was, they always managed to cheer her up. One of the best trips she had was swimming with dolphins in Lapland. She fitted in many experiences that opened up an exciting world to her and let her share in the fun.

She did have many of the same interests as most young girls; she adored the band Queen and went several times to the London show *We Will Rock You*. But she was remarkably mature, thought deeply about injustices in the world and had an unshakeable faith. Jade had time for people of all ages and took a real interest in their lives. She once told one of her carers, "You look really tired. You work too hard. I think you need to take more care of yourself." An old head on young shoulders; that was our Jade, in many ways stronger than any of us!

This concern for others was genuine and deeply felt and blurred the edges between adult and young person, carer and patient. She met everyone on equal terms. You could see this especially when she went to her favourite place, Little Bridge House. It was a very special place for us all and I miss it to this day.

She loved it there and would mark off the days between visits on a calendar. We all loved it and had some fantastic, fun times. It was a place where we all felt completely relaxed. Over the years the staff became trusted friends. Again she showed a maturity beyond her years, accepting the fact that she sometimes had to have a new carer who might not know about her condition or usual routine. She would always spend time explaining what needed to be done and would take as much interest in getting to know them as they her. Of course, she had her favourites who she'd tell all that had been going on in her life, but would want to catch up on what had been happening to them too.

Jade died as she had lived, with no fuss, just the comment that she was so very, very tired.

In spite of it being just five years, it can often feel like yesterday. I miss her more than I can say and no day goes by without me thinking about her. So many things remind me of her, it may be something I do or see, a smell or a sound. I miss her positive outlook on life. I miss, too, having her around to sort me out! She was very organised and would write me a to-do list, to make sure I remembered all the essential things.

She was such an important part of my life that I don't expect to get over losing her, but I carry with me much of what she taught me. One lesson I try hard to remember is not to complain about small, trivial things; they really don't matter. But most of all, through her bravery, Jade taught our whole family not to take life for granted but to be thankful for each day that comes. She also showed us to be kind to others. We have all learnt from her example and we were all so lucky to have had her with us, even for a short time.

Writing this has been hard and there have been many, many tears but it has also been a lovely thing to take time to remember the sweet, brave girl she was and celebrate her life.

Santa Claus *by Jade*

The Curtains Are Drawn
The Lamps Go Down
The Doors Are Locked
The Windows Are Closed

The Fire's Died Down
The Music Is Off
The Christmas Tree Is Dark

The Children Are Sleeping
The Dogs Sleeping
The Cats Purring
The Mice Come Out To Play

The Tap Is Dripping
The Wind Is Tapping
The Cars Drive By

Hear A Jingle
Hear A Rustle, Hear A Rattle
Hear Tapping Hooves

Open An Eye See A Shadow
Open An Eye See Gold Dust
Open An Eye See Someone With A Sack
Open An Eye See Someone Packing Toys
Open Both Eyes And He's Gone
Filled Your Sack And Off He Goes

Everol
By Siobhan

A loving childhood, you can't beat it. It's there for ever and, no matter what life slings at you or however violently you react to events, in the end it leads you gently back on track and helps you find your way. It's your roadmap for life.

I grew up in Ireland, a remote little spot beneath the Galtee Mountains. With my sisters and brother, we led a carefree, idyllic life, fetching water from the spring, playing among the fields and walking the hills. It was a simple existence but we wanted for nothing, except perhaps an inside lavatory. But what you've never had you don't miss and we were just content to revel in the freedom and the beauty of it all. Mum cooked and cleaned while Dad, a bit of an entrepreneur, spent his time wheeling and dealing. We weren't really too sure what he did but we knew he bought and sold greyhounds. He'd go off to England most weeks and as soon as he'd left home I'd want him back again. I was the youngest you see, and his favourite.

After a few years he decided we needed a proper house in a less isolated spot. He'd made his money and his family deserved the best. We moved to a village closer to Tipperary, where an architect designed us a house the likes of which the local people, and us, had never seen before. A big stone building with a drive leading up to it, with a proper bathroom – not only with a toilet but also with hot and cold water that came out of taps. We had electricity for the first time and we kids ran about the house turning on all the lights just for the fun of it. We were in heaven. In spite of our new-found wealth my grandparents in England continued to send us chocolate every week, as they had always done, and we shared this with our new friends, the village children, who thought us very grand. We were popular and life was good. But all this was to change when one morning, as I was leaving for school, I spotted a suitcase in the hall. On our return that afternoon we were told our mother had left, gone off with some chap in the village, and I was not to see her again for several years.

I was nine and the idyll was over. Dad was inconsolable, and at night we could hear his sobs throughout the house. What our mother had done was shameful as far as the neighbours were concerned and we were the talk of the village. Dad took to drink and, even though my eldest sister Bernadette did her very best, the house soon looked neglected and a far cry from the beautiful, happy home it had once been. She tried to step into Mum's shoes but we were having none of it. Thinking back, I realise that it was at that point the seed of resentment was planted deep within me. With hindsight I understand that, for our Mum, this must have been such a hard decision. She really loved us and it must have torn her apart to leave us as she did. But, back then, although I loved and missed her, I was so angry at what she had done to Dad, who was now barely recognisable as the gentle loving man he had once been.

Time passed in a kind of limbo. Then, one night, Dad woke us up to say we must go at once to Bristol as Granddad was dangerously ill and Nan needed us. We couldn't wait till morning or say goodbye to our friends; we must catch the ferry that night. I was in a bit of a daze by the speed of it all, but I do remember clearly crossing the Severn Bridge and being transfixed by the multicoloured lights shining through the darkness. They were magical to me since I had never been anywhere outside my village and we didn't even have traffic lights there, let alone street lighting. An entirely new world was opening up before me.

Nan lived in a quiet residential area of Bristol. She and Dappy had always been comfortably off and she was never expected to do anything but cook delicious meals and entertain all the aunts, uncles and cousins around the family table. So she was lost with him lying helpless and dangerously ill in the downstairs front room. Delighted, and relieved, to see Dad at the door with his band of unruly youngsters, she hugged us until the breath was almost squeezed from our bodies. Dappy lay motionless in the narrow bed, yellow as butter, but still managing a faint smile as, in turn, we kissed his hollow cheek. He died a few days later, surrounded by his loving family. The curtains were pulled tight shut and there he stayed until the day of the funeral, as was the custom then.

My father made it plain to us all that we could not now return to Ireland but must stay here to look after Nan. We moaned a bit about leaving our friends but we knew family came first and so that was that.

It didn't take too long for me, a young teenager and a bit rough round the edges, to find suburban life stifling. Even going to the shops, I was constantly being urged to watch my language and be polite. I began to rebel and finding out that my mother lived in Cardiff demanded to see her. Soon, I was visiting her regularly and, although initially thrilled to see her, I was aware of the deep-seated resentment I felt towards her for leaving us as she did. However, for the moment I was more than happy to trade these feelings for the excitement of multicultural Cardiff.

I was thirteen and my hormones were raging. The clothes, the exotic food and music, people speaking with all kinds of different accents; I embraced them all and in no time was living in the heart of it with Mum.

Dad put up a fight to keep me. "You're the brightest of them all, don't disappoint me!" he pleaded, but I wasn't listening. He even went to court, but I was adamant; this was where I wanted to be. Headstrong and wild, it didn't take me long to start skipping school and hanging out with the wrong gang, getting into everything. Mum soon realised she couldn't control me and I was put into care where, at approved school, I met a black boy and, at the age of 15, became a mum myself.

The relationship turned out to be a disaster. He was violent and I spent much of my time in the local refuge, too proud or too stupid to accept offers of help from the family. A year later Nan died. This was a real shock and, although I could never have lived with her, I did love her and perhaps this made me think again about my loving family. The result was I moved in with my sister. By this time, young as I was, you would have thought that experience would have taught me something, but ...

Still wayward and directionless, I got into a relationship with a Jamaican. He was kind, but he was a rover and certainly not one to settle down. I soon realised the last few years had taught me nothing and, once more, I was alone, giving birth to a baby boy who, although I did not know it then, was to change all our lives. I called him Everol.

Carrying Everol, I always sensed that there was something wrong, but nothing had shown up on the scans or blood tests and I was constantly being reassured that all was 'normal'.

However, at the end of a long and difficult labour my doubts were confirmed. My baby was in the wrong position, facing upwards and blue. Immediately, I was surrounded by a team of concerned obstetricians. When Everol was turned over I saw why. He had a gaping wound at the base of his spin and I was told he had severe spina bifida.

I can remember my heart sinking at the thought that my son was now condemned to a life of disability. I thought of four-year-old Antony, at home, eagerly awaiting a new brother to play with and knowing that that could never be. But Everol was beautiful, so beautiful. His face and hair were perfect and, as I looked down on him, I vowed to be with him always, no matter what. He needed me but I, too, needed him. At nineteen I was young, but I had learnt to speak up for myself. So, right away, I started telling the professionals my baby was going nowhere without me. Plans to move him to ITU baby ward were shelved and an incubator was put next to my bed, where I could see him at all times. I felt fiercely protective of him.

His father visited us once. He was stunned and probably disappointed by what he saw. His comment as he was leaving was supposed to be reassuring, "They'll be able to fix him up." But we both knew that wasn't true. The prognosis was grim; the specialist told me bluntly that there was no point operating to close the hole in his back as he would not survive more than a few weeks. They've a way with words these men!

And so, armed with packets of saline dressings, I took my baby home.

The three of us survived somehow. I quickly learnt on the job, so to speak, never separated from my boys. One morning, determined my baby would not be kept shut away, we went to nursery school with Anthony. I was taught a harsh lesson there about the way the world often views disability. The mothers were chatting and admiring their babies kicking and gurgling on the floor while the toddlers played happily in a corner. Anthony ran towards them and I went to join the mums. But as I stepped forward I was swiftly intercepted by one of the organisers. "I wouldn't put your little one down," she whispered, smiling sympathetically, "he might upset the other mothers." I left at once, Everol in one arm and Anthony's hand clasped firmly in the other. On the way out I caught sight of a poster of a bonny six-month old sitting up and smiling. I knew Ev would never be able to do that and my anger turned to tears.

At three weeks he was very ill and taken to the hospital. I remember one of the nurses saying to me, "You're a young woman, but the pressure of caring for him 24/7 will age you ten years." At home I looked at myself in the mirror and thought, "That's what you think." Turning to Ev I said, "We'll show them!" But my love for Everol was no match for his cruel condition and soon we faced a major crisis. Ev was rushed into hospital and not expected to live through the night. From my bed beside him I looked at his small, grey face peeping above the cover in the incubator. I felt utterly helpless. I didn't have any idea how much or how little Ev understood, but I talked to him anyway – I still do – and so, quietly, I told him, "Listen, I haven't loved you long enough. I'm not ready to let you go."

As I touched his face I felt my life force passing from me to him.

"Please stay!" I begged him.

The following morning there he was, eyes open and curious, as the astounded doctors and nurses fussed round him. This was the first of many 'miracles' Everol performed to confound the professionals and their predictions. He'd performed a miracle on me too. He'd turned an immature, mouthy rebel into a devoted and thoroughly responsible mum. The next thing I did will, perhaps, belie this statement. On the surface it will seem impetuous and stupid, but believe me, I had thought it through.

Having Everol was meant to be; I knew that and I rejoiced in his being mine. But I found that I was always fighting for others to accept him, and this was hard. I know that having given birth to a severely disabled child many parents would decide not to have any further children, just in case, but this wasn't how I felt at all. What I did feel was that I was somehow responsible for the way Ev was, that I had messed up and I knew I had to put it right. I was determined to do everything by the book this time and so, eleven months after Everol was born, I gave birth to a beautiful baby girl, Kizzannie. She was perfect in every way and, like me, loved Ev. Right from the very start, she would do all the things he couldn't do. She brought the sunshine back into my life, even though I was alone again. Bringing up the three of them on my own was not easy, there was very little money, but we got by. I had two cleaning jobs and helpful friends. In many ways this was a good time, in spite of the constant worries about Ev's health. I have fond memories of the babies sitting side by side on the couch, Kissy not yet 12-months-old pushing herself towards Ev and wedging her little body against his so he'd sit up straight and not fall over.

But I was on the rebound and still very vulnerable. Although I didn't realise it then, looking back, I was desperately searching and hoping for someone with whom I could settle down and enjoy a real family life. I didn't see then what I know now so, when I met a man who was kind to me, took me out and wanted to marry me, that was enough. I thought my dreams had come true. I could see, spread out before me, a secure future for us all, so I said yes. It was a terrible mistake. What I had taken for social drinking turned out to be a full-blown problem. He was an alcoholic and, once drunk, became threatening and violent. A catalogue of disastrous events followed and our dysfunctional life meant that, with Everol on my hip and the children in tow, we were back once again at the women's refuge. It took a terrible car crash for me to finally admit this marriage was over.

I now had a fourth child, Terisha. A whole family of my own but, again, it was just the children and me. When would I have that settled life I craved?

Somehow, we still maintained a sense of optimism. Tomorrow was always going to be better and who knew what was waiting for us just around the corner? Thinking about it, I suppose I was harking back to the early years of my childhood, which taught me to trust in the fact that if you did your best for your family, out of love, in the end all would be well.

Throughout this turbulent, chaotic time there was one constant in my life, Everol. He was always there, needing me to see that his complex needs were met and his medication given on time, regardless of what else was going on. Little did I know that he was in charge of the roadmap and pointing me in the direction of my future career. At that time all I knew was that we must get away and go where the children would be safe.

It was my dear sister Angela who came to our rescue once again. It was she who spotted a derelict house as we were out in the car. It looked abandoned, but on enquiry we found it belonged to the council. They were happy to let us have it and adapt it to Ev's needs, if we were prepared to wait. The kids and I were in heaven, a place of our own at last.

Angela was always there for me. She had been my mainstay in the difficult crisis years and I could not have coped without her. We were so alike, even though she was fair whereas I'm dark, and we shared the same quirky sense of humour. We were typical sisters though, falling out sometimes but making up soon after. But she changed when her little son David died. Although she already had two lovely boys, she was never the same again. She lost her way entirely and there seemed to be nothing any of us could do. Some years later, still young, she died tragically. Her sudden death left us all reeling from the shock of it. I miss her still.

While all this had been going on I faced another crisis with Everol. He had stopped eating and had to have a gastrostomy fitted. I felt a failure when this happened because he had always enjoyed his food and this represented yet another loss for him. Because he was never expected to live, I found myself continually fighting for what I saw as essential treatment to improve his day-to-day life. At one point, when I was alarmed by his head growing noticeably bigger, I got him to hospital and demanded they operate to release the pressure from the fluid on his brain. They refused at first and many weeks and months went by before a shunt was finally fitted. By this time the brain damage had already been done. Ev spent six months in hospital. It was a hard time for us both as I stayed beside him and witnessed his pain. On top of it all he contracted MRSA, which just prolonged the agony.

I did fight as hard as I could for my son but didn't, unfortunately, have the experience I have now. Times have mercifully changed and the way this condition is viewed and treated is very different these days.

Before this episode Everol's health had stabilised and he had had a few good years. Home life was full of activity and noise, which he loved. The children included him in everything, the younger ones taking delight at sitting on him in his chair for a ride. During the day he went to an excellent school, where he was really loved by the staff who looked after him and hardly seemed to notice his poor, twisted body. I always took particular care of his personal appearance. He was such a good-looking boy and with his tanned skin, dark hair and deep brown eyes everyone loved him – or was it the smell of Joop, his trademark aftershave that attracted them? Whichever it was, it certainly worked for the dinner ladies! Three of them eventually became his respite parents and continued to look after him until the end. Their devotion to him was incredible and I couldn't have coped without them. I will never be able to thank them enough.

Everol did have some really terrible times that were very challenging but he also had some brilliant ones too. That's life isn't it? Everol inspired loyalty. When in real pain he would still summon up a smile and when the family and special friends came round he'd laugh and 'sing'. He loved music and I would often take him to the theatre. On one occasion, watching *Mary Poppins*, he sang along with the songs so loudly I had to put my hand over his mouth. I thought he'd get us thrown out. He loved these trips and certainly knew how to enjoy himself.

Later on we were referred as a family to Little Bridge House, the children's hospice. This was a very special place, particularly for

Everol and his siblings. We all love to be spoilt and the staff were experts in spoiling us all.

At 18 he moved to St. Peter's Hospice where, although his complex care was difficult, we met the most brilliant doctor. The difference this can make to a family is incalculable. His understanding and practical advice replaced the usual dire predictions. He was wonderful. Jessie May and the lifetime nurses also provided much appreciated support, which in the near future was to prove so vital.

I was in my mid-thirties at this time and, with my dear friend Betty living close by, we were all doing fine. Betty had a son, Gary, and he and I had known each other for years and had an easy-going, sort of brother–sister relationship. We got on well and he had a way with children. When he came to the house we were always pleased to see him. However, that changed when he asked me to go with him to his brother's wedding. I had serious reservations. What would Betty think? I hesitated, and discussed it with her before giving Gary my answer. She was fine about it, I did go and, as they say, the rest is history! Eventually, he moved in and we got married and this time I knew I really had made the right decision.

As the years passed my family came back together. Experience had taught me that none of us should judge another's actions, after all, we never know all the reasons. And so Mum and I put the past behind us and the love that we had felt when I was a child was rekindled. Dad, living in Ireland with his new wife, visits whenever he can and it pleases me to see the affection he and Mum still have for each other. I think I'm still his favourite!

Everol grew into a young man, the very heart of this big family.

As he got older Gary had the wisdom to see he needed, in so far as it was possible, to have his independence and, to maintain a healthy relationship, that the family needed to treat him as a young adult. When he shaved him in the morning Gary would talk to him about all kinds of things and Ev's eyes would tell him how he felt. If some well-meaning visitor came in and went to smother him with kisses, as they had always done, Gary would see Ev's expression and tactfully remind them that Everol was 18 now, and probably past all that.

Our son Tom was born and he completed the family. Gary was with me and for the very first time I felt truly loved and supported. He gave me a new confidence and one evening, when we were watching a television programme about a baby unit at a local hospital, he turned to me and said, "You're a born carer. You'd make a brilliant midwife." There was a short silence before he looked at me and added, "You would, you know you would." My first thought was of Everol. How could I embark on a career that involved years of study, first at college to get my A levels and then University, and look after him? But one of Gary's great strengths was that he never saw Everol as a problem and so he convinced me it really was do-able. The very next morning I went down to the local college and signed on for their Access course. My future career was about to begin.

Everol was always my first priority, but looking at him, a young man, I had to face the hard fact that he was not always going to be here. He was the centre of my life and my first and last thoughts on waking and sleeping were always of him. I had seen him battle for life over the years and perhaps it was that struggle that now made me aware of the value of my own life. I had brought him to adulthood on my own and together we had defied the diagnosis; now perhaps it was my time. I spent one evening at his bedside telling him about my future career and I was sure he wished me well.

This was a very different conversation from the one I was forced to have with him a few months earlier. For some time Everol had made it plain how much he hated having to be in hospital and of late we had seen him struggling more and more. As a family we had taken the difficult decision to agree to a no resuscitation policy if another real crisis occurred. I had told him at that time that it was no longer about me, not anymore, but about him. "I'll keep you out of hospital as long as I can and leave it now for you to decide when you need to leave us."

That said, I had given him a hug and left. I just managed to make it through the door before collapsing in a heap, sobbing. But I knew, however painful it was to make such a decision, I had a responsibility to draw the line somewhere. I knew he would understand and know when he'd had enough. I trusted him.

He knew when he was needed. He was sitting beside me, urging me on when I was completing my dissertation and he was at my side when I finally graduated. Would I have done it had he not been there? I don't know, but his quiet presence saw me through the most difficult times and made me feel that this was something I had to finish, for him as well as for me. He had given me back my life all those years ago and being with him, caring for him, had determined the direction I would finally take. I am now a fully qualified midwife.

Everol died on 18 October 2013, aged 27. During his last nine years he was relatively well, with only a few short admissions to hospital. In my heart I knew he had decided he wasn't going anywhere until I was all right. So now it's up to me. He has moulded me into the person I have become and I won't let him down.

Mum is still living close by. She has been my rock in the last few years, supporting me while I was completing my degree and helping with Everol whenever she could. The tie between us has been tested over time but I know that the love that binds us now is that same love we shared all those years ago in Ireland.

I had lived under the shadow of Everol's death since his birth, but this made his passing none the easier. It is five months now and I am still overwhelmed by his loss, but I am fortunate to be surrounded by my family and with their help, and most importantly Gary's love, I know I will eventually come to realise, like Everol, that however challenging it may be, life really is worth living.

I am going to leave the last word to Gary:

Everol needed round the clock care and, knowing this, some people have recently commented: "At last you've got the time to do exactly what you want."

The truth is, I miss looking after him. It was hard work, but so satisfying. That may sound strange but Everol was such a remarkable kid, being with him was a masterclass in how to live. He educated me to appreciate what I have and what I can do because, unlike him, I'm lucky enough to be healthy. Working with him was a daily reminder of this.

To have helped care for such a courageous young man was a real privilege and I'd do it all again.

"I HAVE KNOWN SHADOW
I HAVE KNOWN SUN
AND NOW I KNOW
THESE TWO ARE ONE."

- RUDYARD KIPLING

Supporters

Every effort has been made in the time available to include everyone who should have been included, but our sincere apologies if anyone has been missed out. Thank you to all who gave anonymously.

Andrews, Vicky	Hamlen, Annette
Barber, Ann and Chris	Hammond, Beryl
Bawdon, Lisa	Hann, Philippa
Bransfield, John	Harper, Mel
Brend, Richard	Hase, Barbara
Burnett-Hitchcock, Charles & Primrose	Hendy, Jane
Burnett-Hitchcock, Jake	Hendy, Mollie
Burtt, Nigel	Hennessy, Fiona
Cairns, Wendy	Hick family
Caley, Tracey	Holme, Alice
Cann, Mark	Holme, Dr Charles
Cann, Val	Holme, Frances
Chinnock, Jo	Hope, Emily
Clark, Natalie	Hudson, Diana
Clarkson's Independent Funeral Directors Ltd	Humphreys, Diana
Clayton, Gangamai Mary	Jakeways, Viv
Collier, Terri	Jennings, Ron and Sara
Collins, Patricia	Johnstone, Drummond
Cotter, Janet	Johnstone, Rachel
Craig, Lisa	Johnstone, Will and Leanne
Davey, Fiona	Julian, Sylvia
Davey, Indi and Robin	Kane, Karen
Dickson, Beverley and Paddy	Kembrey, Chris
Ebanks, Chaim	Kembrey, Dora
Edusei, Steph	Kembrey, Julie
Explorium.co.uk	Kerslake, Sophie
Farrell, Matthew	Lansdowne, Maiya
Foster, Marina	Lansdowne, Megan
Francis, Anna, Andy and Rosa	Lett, Nicholas
Garlick, Jaquie	Llewellyn-Jones, Rachel
Goodden, Michael	Loveday, Daniel
Gunn, Sarah	Lyne, Kate and Andrew

Supporters

Lyne, Sam
MacMullen, Ciara
Marmont, Mike
Martin, Liz
Matthews, Peter
Mazey, Roger
Moore, Barry
Moss, Suzanne
Mustard, Tracy and Kevin
Newton, Chris and Roy
Paget, Dr Amelia
Pavey, Josie and Penny
Perry, Jean
Pibworth, Scott
Pickersgill, Miranda
Pilling, Tracey
Pitt, Leanne
Price, Jeanne
Quick, Claire
Rowe, Teresa, Sam and Sophie
Rybka, Stefan
Ryman, Matt

Savage, Beth
Selley, Clare and Peter
Shakspeare, Alison
Simons, Peter and Hildegard
Simons, Shane
Smale, Sue
Smith, Johno
Smith, Trisha
Telfer, Catriona
Thomas, Andrea
Tily, Kitty
Walker, Alyson
Wall, Mark
Waller, Jacqui
Ward, Jenny and Pippa
West, Brenda
White, Cilla
White, Rohan
Whyte, Shirley
Wilkes, Ann and John
Williamson, Sue
Woodward, Claire

Lives Worth Living was funded through the generosity of people who pledged for 'rewards' to our Crowdfunder project, some anonymously, and those who gave money as gifts.

Our thanks to those who provided 'rewards' for the crowdfunding pledges.

Amy Newton www.amynewton.com
Billy Bragg www.billybragg.co.uk
Strata Books www.stratabooks.co.uk
Alison Shakspeare www.shakspeareeditorial.org
Fiona Prideaux
Exeter Bookbinders www.exeterbookbinders.co.uk
Little Bridge House www.chsw.org.uk/little-bridge-house